A LIFE ALIGNED

THE JOURNEY TO ALLOWING THE MAGIC IN YOUR LIFE

REVISED EDITION

DR MARK A ARCURI

A Life Aligned
PRESS

Published by A Life Aligned Press
Santa Fe, New Mexico

Cover art by Uriel Ramírez.

ISBN 979-8-9946717-0-2 (paperback)

Library of Congress Control Number: 2026901999

TABLE OF CONTENTS

ACKNOWLEDGMENTS

This book is the result of many quiet conversations, unseen supports, and moments of grace that accumulated over time. While my name appears on the cover, *A Life Aligned* was never created alone.

First, my deepest gratitude goes to those who trusted me with their stories. My clients and students have been my greatest teachers. Through your courage, honesty, resistance, breakthroughs, and questions, you shaped the very heart of this work. You allowed me to witness what alignment looks like in real life, not as an ideal, but as a living, imperfect, and deeply human practice.

I am profoundly grateful to the friends who have walked beside me through the many spirals that led here. Those who listened without trying to fix, who reflected me back to myself when I forgot, and who gently held space while I found my footing again. You know who you are.

To Carlos, thank you for your steady presence, your patience, and your deep trust in my timing. You have been a grounding force, a collaborator, and a quiet witness to this unfolding. Your belief in me often arrived before my own did.

I am deeply grateful to my editor, Sonia Castleberry, for her care, discernment, and thoughtful presence throughout this process. Her ability to honor my voice while helping the work become clearer, more spacious, and more itself was an invaluable part of bringing this book into being.

I also want to acknowledge Uriel Ramírez, whose artwork graces the cover of this book. His ability to translate the essence of this journey into image, capturing the spiral, the movement, and the quiet depth of becoming, was nothing short of extraordinary. The cover does not merely introduce the book; it reflects it, holding the spirit of *A Life Aligned* before a single word is read.

To my colleagues and mentors, past and present, thank you for the ways you challenged me to think more deeply, practice more honestly, and remain faithful to the human heart of this work. Your influence lives between the lines of these pages.

I also want to acknowledge the land and people of México, particularly Querétaro, where much of this revision took shape. Living here has softened me, slowed me, and invited a deeper listening. This place has offered not just refuge, but perspective, and I carry that gratitude daily.

Finally, to you, the reader. If you found your way here, something in you was already listening. Thank you for your willingness to pause, reflect, and consider what alignment might mean in your own life. It is an honor to walk alongside you, even briefly, on this part of the journey.

With gratitude,

Mark

INTRODUCTION: THE SPIRAL OF TRANSITION

As you begin, let these words open the doorway to your own unfolding...

> "Life can only be understood backwards, but it must be lived forwards."
>
> — SØREN KIERKEGAARD

> "And the day came when the risk to remain tight in a bud was more painful than the risk it took to blossom."
>
> — ANAÏS NIN

Nearly twenty years have spiraled by since I first wrote *A Life Aligned: The Journey to Allowing the Magic in Your Life*. Looking back, I see myself, earnest, searching, hopeful, not yet fully acquainted with the depth and complexity that life's unfolding journey would reveal. I have changed since then. And, perhaps, so have you.

I am now writing these words as an immigrant in México. I intentionally chose the term immigrant because the language we use can quietly shape how we feel about our own journeys. You may discover, as I did, that naming your experience can open unexpected doors, both inside and out. While expat often softens the reality of relocation for those of us with privilege, painting it as a chosen adventure, immigrant carries a different weight. It speaks to the vulnerability of uprooting, of leaving behind the familiar, of learning to belong and to contribute in a place that may not always understand or welcome you. It is not just a matter of semantics. For me, it is a matter of heart and justice. To call myself an immigrant is to stand in solidarity with all who cross borders by choice or necessity, especially at a time when the United States, my home country, is wrestling with deep questions of division, belonging, and who is allowed to call a place home.

Here in México, I am surrounded by beauty, warmth, and a kind of sanity and simplicity that sometimes feels revolutionary. There are days when I feel the gentle ache of grief for what I have left behind; a certain sense of home, familiar landscapes, and dreams that once felt permanent. And yet, there are moments when gratitude and new belonging arrive quietly, often when I least expect them.

This sense of possibility has only deepened as I witness history unfolding. México has elected its first woman president, Dra. Claudia Sheinbaum, a leader whose approval ratings soar above 80 percent as I write this. President Sheinbaum is not only deeply competent and compassionate, she brings a commitment to equity, science, and the well-being of her people, a balm in an age of cynicism. As a climate scientist and as a person of Jewish heritage in a predominantly Catholic nation, she embodies what becomes possible when diversity is honored and leadership is rooted in knowledge and inclusion. Her election is a genuine source of hope for many, a reminder that real change is possible, that integrity and expertise matter, and that a country can move forward when its people feel seen, valued, and inspired.

I cannot help but contrast this with the heartbreak I feel watching the United States of America struggle with division, fear, and the erosion of values I once believed unshakeable. The contrast is stark: Here, I witness a nation embracing the possibility of new leadership and genuine progress, while my former home grapples with questions of belonging and the very meaning of democracy. In México, I have found not just a new place to live but a renewed sense of what community and courageous leadership can look like.

Life here, of course, is not without its challenges. No place is perfect. But I find myself breathing easier, noticing the richness of daily rhythms and feeling grateful for the moments of belonging and community that find me. And still, I carry grief: the grief of watching my home country become less recognizable, more divided, and for many less safe and less free. I mourn the loss of what home once meant, even as I discover new possibilities for belonging in this land that welcomes me and invites me to slow down, breathe, and remember what truly matters.

If you are reading these words, you may find yourself navigating uncertainty too. Maybe you have lost something: a dream, a place, a sense of certainty or identity. Or perhaps you are quietly searching for your own sense of alignment, longing for a life that feels more authentic and whole. Please know that you are not alone in this, even if it sometimes feels that way.

The journey to a life aligned is rarely a straight path. More often it is a spiral, a dance of intention and surrender, hope and heartbreak, vision and revision. We circle back to old lessons only to find we've grown wiser, more spacious, each time around. Sometimes it's not until much later that we realize how much has already shifted.

There are days when magic feels easy and others when simply getting out of bed is an act of courage. Alignment isn't about getting it right all the time. It's about the kindness of returning, again and again, to what is most true for you, right now. And perhaps with each return you'll find it just a little easier, a little more natural, as if your life itself is quietly relearning how to support you.

A Gentle Invitation to Begin Again

I wonder … What if your life could feel not just bearable but beautiful? Not just "good enough" but deeply aligned, inside and out, with who you truly are, right now. As you let these questions settle, notice if small hints of possibility begin to arise, quietly, in their own time and way.

If you are reading this, you are already answering this invitation. Maybe you're weary of feeling stuck, longing for more meaning or direction or simply ready for something new. The desire for a life you love is not selfish, and it is certainly not naïve. It is a call from your truest self, inviting you home.

We often imagine that a new start requires a dramatic leap, but more often it is as subtle as a whispered yes. Even neuroscience confirms this: Our brains are remarkably responsive to the tiniest shifts in attention, intention, and hope. Sometimes, by simply allowing yourself to imagine something new, you begin creating space for change whether you realize it or not.

What I've learned over the years is that it isn't perfection that brings us fully to life. Instead, it is almost always a gentler kind of alignment, living a little more in resonance with your values, trusting your intuition, making space for longing and fear, and moving forward softly, perhaps even before you feel entirely ready. Alignment is not a final destination. It is a living relationship, a quiet practice you can return to, again and again, each time with a bit more ease. When you are aligned, life flows. Ideas, opportunities, and even challenges become invitations to grow, not reasons to shrink.

And perhaps, as you reflect, you'll remember moments in your own life: a single deep breath, an honest conversation, or the courage to say no or yes just when it mattered most. Even if these memories are faint, notice that alignment is always available, always waiting to return to you, again and again.

From Surviving to Thriving

Perhaps you've become skilled at managing your life, ticking boxes, keeping others happy, quietly setting your own joy aside. You might even find yourself believing it's too late to change or that settling for good enough is all that's possible. But what if, even now, there is a way to move toward thriving, not with a single dramatic leap but with a series of small, self-compassionate choices that quietly accumulate over time? Each moment you offer yourself kindness, every time you honor a longing or uphold a boundary, you are tending the seeds of your own growth, often without even realizing it.

Of course, some of us begin with more resources or support than others; privilege and circumstance open or close doors in ways that are not always fair. Still, thriving is not about perfection or circumstance. It is about cultivating aliveness and possibility from wherever you begin. You move toward thriving not in a single leap but in thousands of gentle, compassionate returns. Every act of self-kindness, every time you honor a longing or a boundary, every time you allow yourself to begin again, you are nourishing your own becoming.

Longing as a Guide

What if your longing isn't a problem to fix but instead a compass to trust? What if, even now as you read this, a quiet longing inside you is gently pointing toward possibility, inviting you to notice what's waiting just beyond the edge of the familiar? Our deepest longings are sacred invitations. They are reminders that we are meant for more than simply getting by.

In my early twenties, I dreamed of moving to Manhattan to wait tables and try my hand at acting. I subscribed to *Backstage* and imagined answering casting calls, but I wasn't brave enough to risk my family's disapproval. It took me years to understand that the longing itself was not foolish or misplaced––it was a messenger, gently pointing me toward a wider sense of possibility.

What if, instead of turning away from longing you followed it, even a little, to see where it might lead? Perhaps what you're yearning for is not only possible but is also a glimpse of a greater wholeness, a paradise waiting to be rediscovered, both within you and all around you.

A Life Aligned Is Possible, Even Now

If the world feels noisy or unsteady, know that these are the very conditions in which transformation is not only possible but most needed. You don't need to have all the answers. You only need a willingness to imagine that something different is possible, even now.

This book is designed to meet you exactly where you are. Whatever your circumstances or doubts, you can begin again from here, from now.

The Promise of This Journey

In the chapters ahead, I'll share stories, tools, and practices that have changed my life and the lives of many others–– real, practical steps to move from wishing to doing, from fear to trust, from misalignment to flow. You'll find science to ground the magic, journal prompts, guidance for resistance, and celebrations of every small victory along the way.

This is not a quick-fix book. It's a living companion for your spiral journey, wherever you may find yourself. Return to these pages whenever you need a nudge, a gentle reminder, or a moment of hope.

A Living Invitation

As you open this book, you may sense that I am walking this path right alongside you, not as an expert removed from the messiness of real life but as a fellow traveler who has doubted, longed, leapt, stumbled, and learned, again and again, to get up and trust once more. In your own way, at your own pace, I invite you to do the same.

Every act of honesty, no matter how gentle, opens the door a little wider. So as you continue, you might let yourself wonder how your journey to a life aligned is already beginning, right here, right now, even as you read these words.

With deep gratitude and hope,

Dr. Mark Arcuri

Querétaro, México

2026

1. INTENTION IN YOUR LIFE

Our intention creates our reality.

— WAYNE DYER

THE POWER of Intention

We hear the word intention everywhere, on social media, in therapy sessions, even at the start of a yoga class. But intention is so much more than a buzzword or a fleeting affirmation; it is, quietly, the practice that shapes the very architecture of a life aligned. Sometimes intention acts almost invisibly, as the subtle force that lets us bridge the distance between hope and action, desire and manifestation, often before we even realize we've begun.

Intention is what has carried me through times of uncertainty, especially in those moments when the path ahead was obscured. Whether I was setting out for Florida years ago or, more recently, answering the call to México, intention was always present, an invisible current running just beneath the surface. Sometimes I could barely sense it--a gentle nudge, a soft whisper. Other times, it was the only thing that kept me from giving up.

As you spiral back through your own story, you might notice that intention is more than simply wanting something; it's the energy you bring to each action, every conversation, every choice. Neuroscience now confirms what wisdom traditions have always taught: Where our intention goes, our attention naturally follows. When you set an intention, your mind begins to tune in to possibilities that may always have been there, simply waiting for your notice. Intention becomes the lens through which reality takes shape, and with even a little practice, you become an active participant in the unfolding of your own life.

Modern brain science shows us that even brief moments of conscious intention activate neural networks linked to motivation, learning, and action. When you imagine yourself living into your intention, what researchers sometimes call *mental rehearsal*, your brain responds as if you are already taking those steps. You might find, sometimes quite naturally, that you begin noticing new opportunities, making different choices, building new habits. In this way, intention quietly offers your brain a map for change, turning even the smallest acts of focus into powerful catalysts for growth.

Sometimes intention is the anchor in a storm, a gentle course correction when you feel lost, the quiet declaration that you are willing to show up, even in uncertainty. It isn't always loud or dramatic. Sometimes, it is as subtle as a breath, a word, or a glance at a sticky note reminding you what truly matters.

A PERSONAL JOURNEY: WHEN INTENTION BECAME REAL

I didn't always understand the difference between a goal and an intention. In my earlier years, I set countless goals: "I will have this career by that age, I will live in this place." Sometimes I achieved them, sometimes I didn't, and I often felt oddly disconnected even when I did. There was always something missing, a yearning for deeper alignment, of co-creating with life instead of muscling my way through.

The shift from goal to intention happened gradually, marked by pivotal thresholds. When I began contemplating my move from New Mexico to Florida, the logistics felt overwhelming. I remember the mixture of excitement and dread, especially around rehoming my dog and two cats. At that point, my intention was simply survival: "Let this work out. Let them find the homes they deserve." Yet something in me sensed there was more at play than luck or effort. I began to intend that everything would resolve perfectly, even if I couldn't see how. I started to act as if help was on its way. The very next day, the perfect family called. And just like that, intention became reality.

There was something quietly magical about that experience and also a humbling lesson: Intention is about participation, not control. I had to trust, let go, and allow myself to receive support.

It's easy to believe that if we set a strong enough intention, we can bend life to our will. But real intention invites us to meet life as a partner, not as a force to be managed. Sometimes, the doors that open or the help that arrives aren't what we might have imagined or chosen for ourselves. The practice is to keep showing up, to hold our intentions lightly, and to allow life to respond in ways that may just surprise us.

Letting go of control means making space for solutions you haven't considered, for kindness from unexpected places, for timing that is often not your own. This kind of trust can feel vulnerable, but it is also where the magic happens, where intention becomes a dance between your deepest desires and life's mysterious generosity.

Years later, as I prepared to move to México, I returned to this practice, now with a bit more wisdom. The "thuds" were different this time: a saltwater aquarium that needed a home, the passing of Lola the cat, the uncertainty of living alone in a new country, with a new language. My intentions became a quiet anchor: "May I be open. May I trust that what I need will find me. May I be ready to welcome what comes, even if it surprises me." I set these intentions again and again, sometimes daily, sometimes moment by moment. And as always, it worked, not because every detail went perfectly but because my mindset, my actions, and my openness were in alignment. I was able to see and receive the help that was offered, to notice signs of support (dolphins, friends, a kind gesture from a stranger), to experience grace, even in the unknown.

Looking back, I see that the times I most needed intention were the very times I felt least certain or least powerful. It was precisely in those moments of vulnerability that intention became real, both a prayer and a practice, both a reaching out and a letting go. The more I acted with heartfelt intention, the more support, guidance, and even coincidence flowed into my life. I became a collaborator with life, not its adversary.

WHAT INTENTION IS (AND ISN'T)

Intention is clarity in motion, a living invitation to pause and honestly ask, "What do I truly want, not from fear, not from habit or expectation, but from my own heart?"

Intention isn't magical thinking, nor is it a guarantee that life will unfold exactly as you wish. For me, intention is a way of returning to center, especially when anxiety threatens to take over. Even now, my intentions are often simple: "May I meet today with curiosity." "May I remember that I am supported, even when I feel alone." Some days, intention is simply the willingness to stay present with whatever unfolds. For some, intention might be the resolve to survive a difficult day, or the quiet hope to reclaim a lost sense of self. Culture, family, and life experience shape what feels possible or even safe to intend. Every intention, however humble or bold, deserves respect.

Living with intention means carrying your *why* into every *what*. You might begin your day by setting a gentle intention: "May I be present in my conversations" or "May I offer myself compassion today." If you forget, or lose track, you can always pause and reset, even with a single breath. Sometimes, the most powerful intentions are the smallest and simplest. Unlike wishes or rigid goals, intentions are rooted in the present moment, guiding how you wish to be rather than what you must achieve. The difference is subtle, but transformative: Goals are about arriving; intention is about journeying well.

An intention might sound like, "May I approach this difficult conversation with kindness" or "I intend to bring awareness and gentleness to my body today." Intentions guide the quality of your presence and invite you to show up more authentically, especially when things don't go as planned.

Setting intention isn't about denying reality or forcing outcomes. Instead, it's a gentle invitation to participate more fully, to return to your center, to allow life to meet you halfway. Even in disappointment or struggle, intention gives you a way to relate to the moment with agency and self-compassion.

Prompt

Maybe ask yourself, what intention might you find yourself needing most these days? Perhaps, as you let these words settle, you'll notice some small promise to yourself, one that feels quietly supportive, maybe even before you can name it.

HOW INTENTION HELPED ME SURVIVE, AND THRIVE, THROUGH UNCERTAINTY

The real power of intention has revealed itself most clearly in the hardest times. When I moved to Florida, the path was anything but a straight line; there were moments when nothing seemed to work, when the doubts screamed louder than the vision. In those moments, my intention became a mantra, an act of self-remembering. I would write it on scraps of paper, tuck notes in my pockets, speak it aloud, especially when I wanted to give up.

When I arrived, exhausted and uncertain, I found myself standing on the dock, looking out at the water. The dolphins that greeted me, the very same ones that had surprised me on my first visit, felt like more than a welcome. They reflected my intention back to me, a quiet affirmation that I had been met by life itself. It was as if the universe were whispering, "You set your intention. You trusted. Welcome home."

That moment became a touchstone for the years ahead. When the time came for my move to México, I leaned on the same practice. I set intentions for language, for connection, for resilience. Sometimes, my intention was simply to get through the day, but the practice, small as it seemed, carried me.

Looking back on these transitions, I realize intention was the thread that held me steady. In the chaos of change, it became the ritual that grounded me, like an anchor dropped in uncertain waters or a lantern lit in the dark. I've seen the same with my clients and students: The right intention doesn't erase pain or difficulty, but it does offer a way through. One student I worked with set the intention simply to ask one question in class, even when anxiety made participation hard. Over time, this intention helped her find her voice and, eventually, the confidence to lead group discussions. Intention doesn't promise ease, but it does promise meaning.

During the darkest moments, during illness, loss, or disappointment, intention offers a way to shape your experience from within. It's as if you are telling life, "I am willing to meet you here, even now, as I am." Sometimes, intention is as simple as "May I find a single moment of peace today" or "May I trust that support will find me, even when I feel alone."

In time, you may discover that your intention becomes a lantern too, helping you see just far enough to take the next step and lighting the way, one gentle return at a time.

INTENTION IN THE 5-POINT PROCESS: WHY IT'S THE BEDROCK

You can't skip intention if you want a life aligned. It is the living heartbeat of transformation, the quiet pulse that keeps you moving even when you can't see the path ahead. Vision gives you direction, but intention is the daily invitation to move toward it, one imperfect, human step at a time. If vision is the *what*, intention is the *how*: the energy, mindset, and quiet faith that carry you when the journey feels long, the anchor that steadies you when tides of doubt or distraction try to pull you off course.

Intention is the current running through the entire 5-Point Process, the tuning fork that brings you back into resonance with your truest self. You may have the clearest vision, the deepest longing, the most detailed plans, but without intention your efforts lack the spark that brings them to life. Intention is what transforms abstract dreams into lived reality. It is the fuel that ignites action, the inner compass that keeps you oriented when circumstances shift or challenges arise.

Think of intention as the connective tissue, the thread that weaves every other step together. It turns your commitments into devotion, your awareness into presence, your actions into something meaningful. In times of uncertainty, intention becomes your lifeline, helping you find purpose even in setbacks, resilience in disappointment, hope when the way forward isn't clear. Every time you pause to remember your intention, you reconnect with the deeper *why* that makes your journey worthwhile.

Intention is not about never wavering or getting it perfect. It is about returning, again and again, to what matters most.

Each time you drift or forget, intention gently invites you home, reminding you that every moment is a new chance to realign, to begin again, to infuse your life with meaning and purpose.

THE RELATIONSHIP BETWEEN INTENTION AND VISION

Vision asks, "What do I desire?"

Intention asks, "How will I move toward it today?"

I've learned this the hard way. Sometimes my vision felt crystal clear, but I stalled because I hadn't truly set an intention. At other times, I set intentions but lacked the courage to see or trust my vision. When the two are paired, transformation flows, like two hands joined at the threshold, pulling you forward and keeping you grounded at the same time.

Vision and intention are partners in creation. Vision inspires; intention grounds. Vision calls you forward into the vastness of what could be. Intention walks you there, step by step, breath by breath, especially when the next step feels uncertain. If your vision is to feel more connected, your intention might be to listen with presence or to reach out to someone with vulnerability today. If your vision is to write a book, your intention could be as humble as "I intend to touch the page, no matter what words come."

When vision and intention come together, with vision opening the horizon and intention guiding the next step, real and sustainable change takes root. In your own spiral journey, you may notice that when you feel stalled or uncertain, it helps to pause and ask which one is missing. Am I lacking vision, or am I lacking intention? Both are essential. Vision carries you toward what matters most, and intention brings your energy, presence, and willingness into this moment, right here and right now.

Vision is what stirs your longing, your *why*. Intention is what brings your why into the world, giving it shape and direction, again and again, each time you return.

HOW INTENTION IS NURTURED AND PROTECTED

Community

Intention grows stronger when spoken, witnessed, and supported. Even sharing your intention with one trusted friend, as I did before moving to México, can bring it out of the realm of fantasy and into the world of possibility. There's a quiet magic in letting your intentions be seen, whether in a circle of friends, a supportive community, or even a single, trusted companion. When your intention is witnessed, it gains substance and strength. The spiral of transformation becomes wider, now including others who can hold you accountable, remind you of your why, and celebrate your returns.

Spirit and Ritual

Rituals matter. They turn intention from idea into embodied experience. I light candles, write intentions on notecards, use meditation as a container for my intention. Sometimes the most profound intentions are the quietest: "May I be open to the magic of today." A ritual, however simple, marks a threshold, a moment of pause where you declare, "This matters." Your ritual can be as unique as you are: a walk at sunrise, a favorite piece of music, or three slow breaths before you begin. Let each ritual be a gentle return, a way of coming home to yourself and your intention, again and again.

Compassion for Self

Intention is also held in the way you meet yourself when things are imperfect. There will be days when you forget what you set, or when old patterns take over before you even notice. These moments are not failures. They are simply invitations to return. Each time you come back to what matters, you strengthen your ability to meet your life with greater honesty and presence.

Nurturing intention is both art and practice. More than any specific ritual, what strengthens intention is the inner shift these moments create, a quiet turning toward yourself. A candle, a breath, a softly spoken phrase, each becomes a symbolic doorway, a reminder that you can return to center at any time. The form is never the point. What matters is the quality of presence the moment evokes and the way it helps you gently come home to yourself.

In time, you may find that this simple act of returning becomes its own kind of devotion. You remember your intention more easily. You move through challenges with a bit more softness. You notice support arriving in unexpected ways. This is how intention grows, not through perfection, but through the steady rhythm of remembering and beginning again.

Client Snapshot: The Intention Shift

One of my clients, Sarah, came to me exhausted by what she perceived as failed goals. Her lists and resolutions led only to guilt and a sense of never being enough. Together, we shifted from goal setting to intention setting. Instead of "I must lose 20 pounds," her intention became, "I intend to honor my body and move in ways that feel nourishing." Over time, she discovered more joy in movement, more compassion for herself, and began making choices from love rather than fear. Intention created space for self-kindness and true, sustainable change.

Sarah's story is just one of many. I've witnessed similar transformations when people shift from "fixing" themselves to caring for themselves, from a spiral of self-criticism to a gentle spiral of return. Intention allows the energy of change to move from pressure and perfectionism to curiosity and kindness. It opens the door to lasting transformation by making every step, every attempt, a win.

Others have experienced this shift too:

A student who let go of "I must be perfect" and instead chose, "I intend to meet each assignment with honesty and effort."

A parent who transformed "I need to control my child" into "I intend to be present and loving, even in conflict."

When intention is the anchor, the journey becomes gentler and the outcomes more meaningful. Each step on the spiral is honored, not as proof of perfection but as evidence of willingness and growth. Every return to intention is a quiet act of courage, a reminder that change, at its heart, is a process of coming home.

COMMON PITFALLS AND HOW TO NAVIGATE THEM

Mistaking intention for control: Remember, intention is about alignment, not manipulation. You cannot force outcomes, but you can show up with clarity, commitment, and a willingness to participate in what unfolds. When you notice yourself slipping into the urge to control, pause and remember that intention is an invitation to partner with life, not command it.

Getting stuck in the *how*: If you catch yourself obsessing over logistics or micromanaging every detail, gently return to your core intention. Trust that the details will often sort themselves out, sometimes in ways you couldn't have planned, as they did for me with both pets and new beginnings. Let intention hold the vision, and let life surprise you with its timing.

Forgetting to revisit your intention: Let intention be a living, breathing practice. Revisit and revise it often, allowing it to grow as you do. When you lose touch with your intention, that isn't failure, it's a gentle nudge to return, to begin again.

It's also easy to overcomplicate intention or to let it slip into self-criticism. Notice if your intention starts to feel like a *should*, or an obligation. If it does, pause and return to your heart. Ask yourself, "What truly matters to me right now?" Keep your intentions simple, alive, and responsive to your current needs.

If you find yourself abandoning your intention when you stumble, remember: Each detour is simply another invitation to recommit. The spiral of growth is not about perfection, it's about presence. Every return is meaningful.

Once a week, pause to check in with yourself:

Does my intention still feel inspiring?

Is there a new quality or energy calling for my attention?

How can I refresh my practice so it feels nourishing, not forced?

Let these questions be gentle thresholds, inviting you to deepen your alignment as you continue forward.

Exercise: Your Daily Intention Practice

Begin each day with a quiet moment, perhaps before you get out of bed, or as you prepare for a meeting, a call, or any important event. Ask yourself: What energy, quality, or experience do I wish to bring to this day? It might be courage, curiosity, openness, compassion, or simply presence.

Record your intention in your journal. The act of writing it down gives it form and power. You might even leave space to return and notice how living with this intention gently shifts the course of your day.

At the end of the day, return to your journal and reflect: How did my intention shape my experience? Where did I feel most aligned? Where did I drift? What might I intend tomorrow? Write freely: This is your space to notice patterns, celebrate progress, and gently spiral back to what matters most.

Try this for a week

Each morning, write your intention for the day.

Carry it in your heart or place a reminder such as a sticky note, a phone alert, a stone in your pocket, somewhere you'll see it,

Each evening, check in. Did your intention show up for you? Where did it support you? Where did you forget?

Refine your intention as needed. There's no right or wrong, only honest learning and gentle return.

You may be surprised at how such a small, consistent practice creates real shifts in your day, your mood, your relationships, and your sense of what is possible.

Reflection: Intention and the Aligned Life

How do your current intentions reflect your deepest values and desires?

Where might you set intention instead of a rigid goal?

When in your life have you felt the magic of intention meeting you halfway?

Allow yourself to sit with these questions, not needing to answer perfectly but letting your responses spiral and evolve over time. Revisit your journal often. Sometimes, the true power of intention is revealed only in hindsight as you pause to notice just how far you've come.

Other questions for your reflection:

What does living with intention feel like in your body, your mind, your spirit?

Where in your life could a gentle intention soften the edges or invite more possibility?

When have you experienced a "happy accident" or synchronicity after setting an intention? What did you notice?

Return to your intention any time you feel off course. It is always available, a threshold you can cross, again and again, no matter where you are on your spiral.

THE 5-POINT PROCESS FOR WHOLE LIFE ALIGNMENT: YOUR ROADMAP

As you move forward in this book, you'll journey through my 5-Point Process for Whole Life Alignment, an approach that has evolved through my own lived experience, my work with clients, and the quiet magic that happens when we align with intention. Here's what you can expect as you spiral through each step:

Vision: What do you truly want? This is where the process begins, with the courage to imagine, sense, or claim a life or outcome that truly pings for you, even if you don't yet know all the details.

Commitment: How willing are you to dedicate yourself to your vision? This step is about making the conscious choice to show up for your dream again and again, even when it's hard, inconvenient, or uncertain.

Awareness: How do you relate to what's unfolding? Here, you practice presence. You notice signs, challenges, synchronicities, and the subtle ways you might resist or support your own transformation.

Living Into Your Intention: How do you bring your intention into action? This is where intention and action meet. You act as if what you want is possible, taking small, aligned steps, adjusting course, and learning along the way.

Integration (formerly Living a Life Aligned): How does it feel to live in alignment? This is the ongoing experience of living from your authentic self, reaping rewards, learning from setbacks, and knowing you can return to the process any time you drift from your center.

Throughout it all, intention is the current that runs through every step, a living thread weaving everything together. Setting clear intentions helps you clarify your vision, commit more fully, heighten your awareness, and take actions that truly reflect who you are becoming.

As you continue, let intention be your companion in each phase. Let it remind you that growth is a spiral, not a straight line. Let it offer you grace on the days when things are messy and amplify your joy when things flow. Trust that your intention, even when quiet, is always heard, by yourself, by life, by the field of possibility that surrounds us all.

PREVIEW FOR THE READER

As you continue this journey, we'll explore the foundations that make a life aligned not just possible but inevitable. You'll discover how intention weaves quietly through every area of your life, how to create the space for change, and how each step, no matter how small, prepares you for transformation in your own unique way. For now, let your intention be simple: I am open to discovering what is possible for me.

Before you turn the page, perhaps pause for a breath. Place a hand on your heart and gently say, I am open to discovering what is possible for me. Notice any shift, a spark, a question, or simply a moment of presence. That is intention at work.

The journey continues, one step, one breath, one intention at a time. The spiral awaits.

2. THE ANATOMY OF INTENTION

The future depends on what you do today.

— MAHATMA GANDHI

INTENTION: FROM INSPIRATION TO ACTION

By now, you may have noticed that intention is the invisible force animating every aspect of a life aligned. But what does it really look like in the gentle rhythm of a day? How do you allow intention to move from being a nice idea or feeling into a real, living energy in your life, one that quietly supports you even when you aren't paying attention?

Intention is not just an abstract concept or a spark that fades when life gets messy. True intention transforms longing or wishing into something that shapes your choices, colors your experience, and grounds you, through both triumphs and setbacks. In this chapter, let's explore how to bring intention down from the clouds and root it in your beautiful, imperfect, very real daily life.

Together, we'll break down the anatomy of intention, what it truly is, what gives it power, and the gentle practices that help you spiral from inspiration to action, even when the world feels uncertain or your energy is low. Think of intention as a bridge between inspiration and embodiment, the current running through your everyday life, turning even mundane moments into quiet opportunities for presence, meaning, and transformation. Here, you'll not only learn how to set intentions but, more importantly, how to live them, especially when things don't go as planned.

THE ELEMENTS OF A POWERFUL INTENTION

A meaningful intention has distinct qualities. Each one makes the difference between a fleeting wish and an engine for real change:

1. Clarity

A clear intention is specific about what you want to feel, create, or experience. Instead of "I want to be happier," you might quietly try, "I intend to notice beauty today," or "I intend to bring patience to my conversations." Clarity helps you recognize when you're on track or when you need to gently refocus.

Vague intentions drift away; clear ones serve as internal guideposts. Clarity comes from honesty, naming what you truly want, not what you think you *should* want. You might be surprised how liberating it feels to listen to your own needs and desires, even if they feel inconvenient or unfamiliar at first.

2. **Alignment**

An intention that "pings" is one that resonates with your values, desires, and authentic self. If you set an intention you don't quite believe in, or that belongs to someone else's idea of what's best, it will likely feel hollow, a thud rather than a ping. Pause and softly ask: Does this intention feel true to me, right now?

Alignment is the gentle difference between forcing yourself to try harder and allowing yourself to move into a state of flow. When your intention feels like your own, you're much more likely to stay with it, even when life gets challenging.

3. **Present Tense**

State your intention as if it's already unfolding: "I intend to welcome support today." "I am willing to see this situation differently." Speaking in the present brings the energy of intention into the here and now, inviting your mind and body to participate as if it's already happening. Your nervous system begins to respond in kind, priming you for openness and action rather than waiting for some perfect future moment.

4. **Emotional Charge**

Intention is most powerful when you connect to how it will feel, not just what it will look like. You might ask yourself: If this intention were fulfilled, what would I feel? Then, practice holding that feeling, even for a breath or two.

Emotions are quiet fuel. The more you allow yourself to touch the feeling state of your intention: calm, gratitude, maybe even courage, the more your actions and perceptions begin to align. It's not about forcing yourself to be positive but about giving your intention a spark of real aliveness.

Emotional charge gives intention its power, but the story doesn't end with feeling. Neuroscience shows us that intention is not just a mental act, it's a physical, embodied one. When you anchor your intention in genuine emotion and revisit it, you activate and strengthen neural pathways that support new habits and patterns. Each time you act as if your intention is true, even in a tiny way, you reinforce these pathways, teaching your brain and body what's possible.

Over time, intention becomes less an abstract idea and more a lived experience, something you can sense in your posture, your breath, your energy. These shifts signal to your nervous system that change is underway, making it easier to return to your intention and move forward, even when doubt or old habits tug at you.

5. Flexibility

Release the need for control. Let intention be your compass, not your GPS. Sometimes, life delivers on your intention in ways you never expected or on a timeline not your own. The most resilient intentions are those that adapt and evolve.

Flexibility is the art of showing up with hope and direction while holding everything with humility and openness. Sometimes, what comes is not what you imagined, but it's just what you needed.

THE ANATOMY IN PRACTICE: HOW TO SET (AND LIVE) AN INTENTION

As you begin to craft your own intentions, remember: There is no single right way to do this. Your intentions do not have to be grand, dramatic, or even visible to anyone else. For some, a powerful intention might be as simple as "I will rest when I am tired" or "I will offer myself a kind word today." For others, it might be simply to survive, to persist, or to imagine a slightly softer way of being.

Your family history, culture, current life circumstances, and personal identity all shape what feels possible or safe for you to intend. You have full permission to honor your reality. Whether your intention is to show up in a meeting, ask for help, make art, or breathe through a difficult moment, every intention counts. Progress isn't measured by size or drama, but by your willingness to meet yourself where you are and to claim what matters to you, even in the smallest way.

Begin With Presence

Take a few conscious breaths. Place a hand on your heart or belly. Feel your feet on the ground. Allow yourself to arrive, right where you are. Before any intention can guide you, simply notice how it feels to be present, even for a moment.

Name What Matters

Ask yourself, softly: What do I want to experience, feel, or bring into this day (or situation)? Listen for the answer that pings. Don't rush it. If you wish, pause here and jot down what comes up in your journal. Let honesty be your guide. No one else will see this.

Sometimes what matters most will surprise you. Beneath the drive to get things done, there may be a longing for peace, connection, or courage. Naming this truth, without judgment, is the first gentle step toward living in alignment.

State Your Intention Simply

"I intend to meet challenges with curiosity."

"I intend to notice moments of connection."

"I intend to bring gentle courage to this next step."

Simplicity gives intention power. The more concise and heartfelt your intention, the easier it will be to remember and return to it, again and again.

Write, Speak, or Ritualize

Record your intention in your journal, speak it out loud, or use a small ritual. Light a candle, hold a stone, write it on a sticky note. Rituals give intention a physical anchor, making it more tangible and memorable.

Act As If

As you go about your day, pause and ask, How might I act if my intention were already guiding me? Small actions aligned with your intention create momentum. When you act as if your intention is present, you gently train your mind and body to move in that direction.

Review and Reset

At day's end (or week's end), check in: How did my intention shape my experience? Celebrate any shift, no matter how subtle. Reset as needed. Intentions can evolve. Some days your intention will feel alive. Other days, you'll forget. Both are natural. Each return is a quiet victory, a spiral home-coming to what matters most.

Quick Intention Reset

There will be days when life doesn't offer the luxury of a full journaling session or a crafted ritual. When you feel scattered or off track, try this simple reset:

Pause and place a hand over your heart, or wherever you feel most grounded.

Take a slow, conscious breath.

Silently or aloud, name your intention for the next few minutes or hours, even if it's as simple as "Be gentle," "Stay present," or "Begin again."

This practice takes less than a minute, but it can re-anchor you whenever you need it. Over time, these small resets gently weave intention into the fabric of your everyday life, reminding you that you can always start again, right where you are, one gentle breath at a time.

FROM STUCK TO FLOW: USING INTENTION WHEN YOU FEEL OFF COURSE

We all lose our way sometimes. The quiet magic of intention is that you don't have to be perfect, you simply need to remember and gently return. When you notice anxiety, frustration, or self-doubt, pause and revisit your intention. Maybe you set an intention in the morning but got swept up in busyness or old habits. That's normal. The practice is simply to come back softly.

If you notice yourself feeling off course, take a moment to open your journal and write what you're experiencing. Sometimes, naming the feeling––"I feel stuck," "I feel tired,"

"I'm doubting myself"--can shift the energy all by itself. Then, write your intention again or adjust it if you need to. There is quiet power in seeing your intention in your own handwriting.

When I first moved to México, there were days I felt overwhelmed by language, bureaucracy, or loneliness. My intention for those days became, "May I show myself compassion and reach out for support when needed." On difficult days, I wrote that intention in my journal as a gentle reminder. Sometimes just repeating it or seeing it on the page changed my experience, even if nothing outside me changed.

Your journal is always there to help you gently return to your intention, no matter how many times you drift. Each return is its own act of courage, a quiet step back into flow.

Even when the world outside feels unmovable, your intention remains a living bridge to possibility. With practice, you'll begin to notice how quickly you can course-correct, how the simple act of naming and resetting your intention can open space for a new experience even when everything else stays the same.

PRACTICAL TOOLS: BRINGING INTENTION INTO YOUR DAY

Morning Ritual

Begin each day by setting one small, clear intention. Even if the day ahead is full of uncertainty, let your intention be your anchor. A morning intention can gently shape your mood, focus, and sense of possibility. Sometimes, all it takes is a breath and a single phrase.

Visual Reminders

Place your intention where you'll see it: a sticky note on the mirror, your phone's lock screen, a favorite mug. Surround yourself with visual cues, especially in stressful moments, to keep your intention quietly alive throughout your day.

Mindful Pauses

Set a timer for a few mindful check-ins. When it goes off, ask yourself, "Am I living my intention?" If not, gently reset. These pauses bring you back from autopilot, inviting a conscious, compassionate choice.

Intentional Transitions

Before meetings, calls, or new activities, pause and reset your intention: "May I bring presence to this conversation." "May I listen more than I speak." Transition moments are perfect opportunities to anchor yourself in the energy you wish to carry forward.

Weekly Reflection

Each week, take a few moments in your journal to review the intentions you set. Note what worked, what challenged you, and what you learned. Over time, this reflection reveals patterns, strengths, and growth, offering wisdom you might otherwise miss.

Adding these gentle structures: a morning ritual, a lunchtime pause, or an evening review, turns intention from an idea into a way of being. Consistency matters more than intensity. Let these practices spiral through your days, meeting you right where you are.

Moving from Theory to Action: An Exercise

Take a moment in your journal to do a gentle intention audit. List three areas of your life, such as work, relationships, health, or anywhere else where you feel stuck or want change. For each area, softly write about what you most deeply want to experience.

Then, for each area, craft a present-tense intention:

"I intend to collaborate with ease at work."

"I intend to bring kindness to my self-talk."

"I intend to savor my meals with gratitude."

Choose one intention to live with for the week. Notice what shifts, internally or externally. Let your discoveries be gentle. Change may not be immediate or dramatic. Sometimes, the only sign is a little more peace, a little less resistance, or the quiet courage to try again.

Other times, new insights, opportunities, or synchronicities appear, almost as if by magic.

THE GENTLE ART OF COURSE CORRECTION

It's easy to slip into self-criticism when your intentions seem to fail. But intention was never meant to be a test of perfection. Instead, let every day, and every moment, be a new invitation. Sometimes, the most meaningful intention you can set is simply, "I intend to forgive myself and try again."

Intention is not perfection. It's the art of returning, again and again, to what you value most. True failure isn't in forgetting your intention or drifting off course but in denying yourself the chance to return. The courage to begin again, to reset your focus and recommit, is at the heart of living a life aligned. Every gentle return to your intention is a victory: it strengthens your capacity for presence, for self-compassion, and for trust in your own growth.

When you notice yourself drifting, don't berate yourself. Simply smile, pause, and breathe. Acknowledge your humanity. Your intention isn't lost; it is quietly waiting for you, right where you left it.

If you lose sight of your intention, remember: This is not a sign that you've failed but a natural part of any real transformation. Everyone drifts, forgets, or even resists their own intentions from time to time. What matters most is not how perfectly you stay on track but how gently and honestly you return. You're not starting over each time you begin again. Instead, you are strengthening new pathways in your mind and heart, quietly proving to yourself that you are capable of change and worthy of compassion. Progress is made in these moments of return, not in never getting lost.

Let every return to your intention be a quiet celebration, a sign that you are alive, attentive, and still moving toward what matters most. The spiral of change always welcomes you back.

Reflection: The Anatomy of Your Intention

Take some quiet time in your journal to explore these questions. Let your answers be as detailed or as brief as you wish. They are for you alone.

Which element of intention (clarity, alignment, emotional charge, flexibility) feels most natural for you?

Which feels most challenging?

What is one area in your life where you'd like to practice setting intention more consciously?

How will you remind yourself to return to your intention when you drift?

If you feel inspired, go further: What might shift if you approached your daily life as an ongoing experiment in intention? Where could you invite more curiosity and less self-judgment? What is the most compassionate intention you can offer yourself in this season of life?

Let your reflections spiral and evolve. Remember, every gentle return to intention is a new beginning.

INTEGRATION: WHERE INTENTION BECOMES EMBODIED

As you move ahead, you'll notice intention woven through every step of the process and every story, including your own. Intention is both the invitation and the anchor: it calls you forward and grounds you where you are. With every intention you set, you are quietly building the muscle for a life more fully aligned, one gentle choice at a time.

Integration isn't a single moment of accomplishment but the cumulative effect of returning to intention again and again. Over time, through practice, intention becomes less an effort and more a natural way of relating––to yourself, to others, and to the world. This is the quiet power of integration: when intention moves from concept to lived experience, from theory to a felt sense of belonging and homecoming in your own life.

As you move from the practice of intention into the realities of change, remember: Every day is an opportunity to weave intention into your being. Let it be a gentle, steady companion, one that welcomes you back whenever you stray. In this way, your intentions become not just words or wishes but the living thread that spirals through every chapter, grounding you, guiding you, and inviting you home, again and again.

LOOKING AHEAD: A LETTER FROM MÉXICO

As you reflect on your own intentions, where you have stayed true, where you have drifted, and how you have found your way back, know that you are not alone. This practice of remembering and returning is shared by all of us who are called to live more authentically.

In the next chapter, I invite you to join me for a more personal glimpse into this ongoing journey, through a letter I wrote from México. It is a letter about longing, uncertainty, and the courage to begin again, written not just for myself but for anyone navigating the space between what was and what could be. As you read, may you find resonance, reassurance, and perhaps even the inspiration to write your own letter to yourself as you spiral forward on your path.

As you turn the page, keep your intentions close and your journal open. Integration is born from all these small, courageous acts of remembering and returning. Your life aligned is not a distant dream but a reality you gently build, moment by moment, intention by intention.

The journey continues.

3. LETTER FROM MÉXICO

DEAR FRIEND,

If you find yourself reading these words, you are likely pausing at the threshold of your own new chapter. Perhaps you're feeling a longing for transformation or an uncertainty about the world. Or maybe, like me, you've heard that quiet whisper that it might be time for something more.

I write to you now from my home in Querétaro, México, a place that's become as much a state of mind as a spot on the map. This move didn't happen overnight. In truth, it was a vision quietly held in my heart for years, a dream whose roots took hold long before I allowed myself to speak it out loud. Isn't it interesting how some part of us knows well before we're ready to claim it?

For a decade, I found myself returning to México again and again. I was drawn by the warmth, the colors, the music of life spilling into the streets and weaving through every encounter. There was a longing, a gentle pull toward belonging, but also a sense that the timing was not yet right. Sometimes, life asks us to wait, even as we feel ready to leap. Sometimes, patience is its own quiet kind of wisdom.

People would ask, "When are you finally going to do it?" Honestly, I'd reply, "I think I will, but I have no plans." Deep inside, I just knew there would come a day when I'd wake up and feel with absolute clarity that now was the moment. And just as quietly as the dream began, that moment arrived.

It was early 2024. I was in a business meeting over morning coffee and pan dulce with Carlos, my soul brother and steady companion on this journey. The shift settled in. We sat in a café, open to the world, and a simple knowing unfolded inside me.

Now was the time to allow the next chapter. I turned to Carlos and said, "I'm ready."

He smiled a knowing smile, full of patience and love, and replied, "I know. I was just waiting for you to say it."

There are people in our lives who gently hold space for our becoming, quietly waiting for us to claim what they've sensed all along. Carlos is one of those people for me: steady, gentle, unwavering in his support, trusting my timing even when I doubted myself. In his presence, I learned that sometimes what we need most is not a push but someone who honors our process and holds the vision for us until we're ready to claim it as our own.

Later, I shared my decision with my best friend Chuck in Albuquerque. He, too, simply responded, "I know," and told me about a dream he'd had in which I was stepping into a new chapter. Sometimes, those who truly love us can sense our readiness before we speak it aloud. Their quiet confidence becomes a kind of blessing for the journey ahead, a silent nudge from the universe itself.

Of course, readiness is only the first step. My impulse was to pack up and leave immediately, but Carlos's wisdom and eventually my own prevailed. "You need a six-month plan," Carlos said. And so, I began the slow work of organizing my life in Santa Fe, saying gentle goodbyes, honoring what had been, and opening to what was coming next.

What I'd love for you to know is this: Moving, whether across continents or simply into a new version of yourself, is rarely a straight line. There are moments of vision. There are moments of doubt. Sometimes the universe quietly nudges you forward. Sometimes you must wait, allowing life to catch up with your dreams. And sometimes, all at once, the path opens beneath your feet.

Now, as I look out over the hills from my home office, I'm reminded that every journey worth taking is, at its heart, a journey of authenticity. It is about learning to listen for what is most true and alive in you and allowing that to shape your world, even when the world feels uncertain or out of control. The real magic, I've come to know, is in listening deeply to yourself and honoring the timing of your own life.

So, as you continue on this spiral journey through A Life Aligned, I invite you to wonder gently with me:

What is the "México" in your own life?

What vision has been quietly waiting for you to say, "I'm ready"?

Who are the Carloses and Chucks, those patient, loving souls holding space for you until you claim your next chapter?

Allow yourself, if you wish, to listen, to dream, and, when the moment feels right for you, to say yes. Know that it is never too late. The universe, in its own perfect timing, is always ready to meet you right where you are.

With gratitude for the path that brought us here, and with anticipation for all that awaits,

Mark

Querétaro, México

January, 2026

Every new chapter invites us to show up authentically, even when the world feels uncertain. In the next chapter, we'll explore how authenticity can become our anchor, no matter what storms we face or where the next step leads.

4. AUTHENTICITY IN UNCERTAIN TIMES

To be yourself in a world that is constantly trying to make you something else is the greatest accomplishment.

— RALPH WALDO EMERSON

THE WORLD AT YOUR DOOR: PRESSURES, SEASONS, AND THE CALL TO AUTHENTICITY

THERE ARE seasons in life when the world outside, and sometimes even within us, seems intent on pulling us away from our own center. This pull can be subtle or overwhelming, a steady undertow of expectation, social pressure, or fear that urges us to adapt, conform, or silence ourselves to maintain a sense of safety or belonging. You may feel it in your bones. A quiet tension, a longing for something more honest, or a weariness from trying to fit yourself into shapes that don't quite match your true self.

If you notice this in your own life, you are not alone. In recent years, I've seen this tension everywhere: in global headlines, in the stories of my students and clients, in the shifting ground beneath my own feet. There are mornings when I wake with a question that hums beneath the surface: How do I hold on to my truth in a world that feels so committed to turning me into someone else? This question, I believe, is the quiet call of our age.

We live in a time when division and discord seem to flourish. The old stories of progress and belonging feel less certain, and the noise of the world grows louder by the day. For many, especially those who feel "different" or who walk the margins, the simple act of showing up as yourself has never felt more challenging, or more important.

Emerson's words are a compass here. To be yourself is not simply about self-expression but about the deep, ongoing work of discovering, naming, and standing for who you truly are, even as the world, in a thousand ways, encourages you to forget, to doubt, or to hide. Each day, you are invited to step gently across the threshold of expectation and spiral back toward your own center.

As you begin this chapter, perhaps pause for a moment to notice: Where do you feel the pull of outside pressures in your own life? Where does the call to authenticity quietly tug at you to return?

AUTHENTICITY AS A DAILY REVOLUTION

Let's be honest: Authenticity isn't always comfortable or easy. Some days, the effort to be true to yourself feels like standing in a strong wind, an ongoing negotiation between the pull of belonging and the need to be real. The rewards for fitting in are often immediate: approval, safety, the soothing hum of acceptance. But over time, the cost of that comfort is a quiet erosion of your spirit, a slow fading of your own song.

Authenticity, then, is a daily revolution, a series of small, courageous acts that may be invisible to others but that slowly change the very architecture of your life. Some days, it looks like speaking your truth in a room where silence is expected. Other days, it's the quieter choice: stepping away from a conversation that leaves you depleted, taking time alone to listen for your own voice, or simply saying no to something that drains you.

For me, authenticity has often meant making choices that defy convention: listening to my intuition when the world offered only logic, honoring my need for solitude in a culture obsessed with productivity, naming my identity even when it risked belonging. Each time I chose my own path, I felt both the sting of loss and the warmth of a deeper homecoming. There were moments when I longed to take it all back, to trade discomfort for ease. But every time I returned to myself, the relief was unmistakable.

What about you? Perhaps you too have your own collection of *small revolutions*, moments when you chose to speak up, to walk away, or to hold your ground, even if your voice trembled. These moments, whether noticed or not by others, are the foundation of a life aligned. Each one is a gentle spiral back to center, a quiet affirmation that your truth matters.

THE LONGING FOR BELONGING, AND THE RISK OF LOSING YOURSELF

We humans are wired for connection, for the safety and warmth of community. This longing is both beautiful and dangerous: beautiful because it gives our lives meaning and support; dangerous because, in the absence of true acceptance, we may twist and contort ourselves into versions that are only partly true.

Family, culture, and society all play their parts in shaping our sense of self. Some of us learned early that certain parts of who we are––our feelings, dreams, desires, identities––were unwelcome or even unsafe. We became adept at hiding, pleasing, shrinking, performing. Over time, these strategies became second nature, so deeply embedded that we might not even notice how often we abandon ourselves in order to be loved.

And yet, somewhere beneath the learned scripts and habits of self-denial, there is a current that runs true, a longing for wholeness, for the freedom to be as we are, without apology or pretense. Emerson calls this our *greatest accomplishment*: the refusal to become only what the world demands and the gentle, stubborn return to our own nature.

What has the world, your family, your community asked you to become? What have you given up or hidden to keep the peace? Where do you feel most yourself, and where do you sense the cost of pretending?

As you pause here, you might notice: Beneath it all, there is always a spiral homeward, quietly inviting you back to what is most real.

THE PRACTICE OF RETURNING: YOU, AGAIN AND AGAIN

If you take nothing else from this chapter, let it be this: Authenticity is not a fixed state, not a badge you earn and wear forever. It is a living practice, a gentle process of returning to your own center, especially after you've drifted or lost your way.

Some days you will shine. Your truth will feel clear, your words confident, your presence magnetic. Other days you may be swept up by tides of doubt or the winds of external opinion. This is not failure; it is simply being human.

What matters is the return, the willingness to notice when you have left yourself behind, and to come home once more. Sometimes, that return is a single breath: a quiet pause in your day, a hand over your heart, or a moment of honesty in your journal. It might be the gentle act of naming a longing, even if you're not ready to act on it. Sometimes it's canceling plans you made out of obligation or choosing to spend a quiet evening alone when what you need is rest, not more activity. Perhaps it's letting yourself cry when you've tried to be strong or sharing a vulnerable truth with a trusted friend.

Other times, the return takes the form of a more public gesture: having a hard conversation; drawing a boundary; or stepping away from a situation, job, or relationship that no longer fits. It might even be as simple as changing your mind or saying no when you've spent a lifetime saying yes.

This ongoing coming home is, itself, the accomplishment. Each return, no matter how small, strengthens your capacity for self-trust, for inner guidance, and for resilience in a world that changes by the hour. The spiral of authenticity is not about staying perfectly centered but about remembering, noticing, and returning to yourself again and again, with kindness.

THE PARADOX OF VULNERABILITY AND STRENGTH

There is a myth that authenticity requires confidence, that you must know yourself fully and speak with unwavering certainty. The truth, as Emerson and modern research agree, is that authenticity is often born in moments of vulnerability, not bravado.

To be yourself means to risk being misunderstood, rejected, or dismissed. It means admitting, "I don't have all the answers," or "I'm afraid," or "This is me, flaws and all." Vulnerability is the birthplace of real strength, not its opposite. Each time you allow yourself to be seen, even a little, you invite true connection, not only with others but also with yourself.

Brené Brown's work shows that vulnerability is the bridge between authenticity and belonging. When you let your guard down, you not only become more relatable, you also create the conditions for growth, learning, and healing. Authenticity, then, is a willingness to risk, not recklessly but wisely, choosing where and when to show yourself fully and when to protect what is still tender.

Sometimes, vulnerability opens the door to connection, support, or a new understanding. Other times it may bring discomfort, awkwardness, or even rejection. Both outcomes are part of the spiral. What matters most is how you meet yourself in those moments, honoring your courage and tending to what is tender in you.

Reflection Prompt

When have you allowed yourself to be vulnerable? At work, at home, in love, or in friendship?

What happened? Did it lead to connection, support, or new understanding? Or did it bring discomfort, rejection, or regret?

How did you respond?

What did you learn about your own capacity for courage?

AUTHENTICITY IN THE MICROMOMENTS: SEEDS OF A LARGER REVOLUTION

If you imagine authenticity as a grand act, you might overlook the quieter places where it takes root. Every day, you are offered countless opportunities to return to yourself, some dramatic, but most small and easily missed:

Saying no when you need rest, even if others expect a yes.

Letting your true laughter or honest tears be seen.

Speaking a difficult truth, gently, to someone who matters.

Taking a walk alone when your soul needs quiet.

Admitting you don't know and asking for help.

Each microact of authenticity is a seed. Over time, these seeds become a garden, a place where your spirit can breathe, grow, and offer shade to others. And every garden needs tending. If you forget, forgive yourself. Begin again, as many times as needed. The spiral always welcomes you back.

Try This

List five small acts you could take today to honor your truth. They might be as simple as a pause, a word, or a decision to let something go. Choose one to practice and notice how it shifts your day, even in the smallest way.

The Shaping Power of Family and Culture

Our earliest lessons in authenticity (or its opposite) come from family and culture. Some families teach that difference is dangerous, that dreams must be practical, that feelings should be hidden, or that love must be earned. Others celebrate uniqueness, encourage expression, and make space for honest dialogue.

No matter where you started, you now have the chance to notice which stories, beliefs, and rules are truly yours to keep and which you may be ready to gently release. This is a lifelong process, often filled with moments of grief, relief, and surprise.

I have had difficult conversations with my own family, navigating differences in values, identity, and politics. Sometimes these conversations end in silence or distance. Other times they bring new understanding or a tentative peace. What I have learned is that authenticity rarely leads to a tidy resolution. Instead, it asks us to tolerate the discomfort of difference and to stand kindly in our own truth, even when belonging is not guaranteed.

For many, the work is not about a single "coming out" or public declaration but about a series of daily negotiations. You might quietly ask yourself: What can I safely share? What must I protect? When is it time to risk, and when is it time to wait? If you have walked this path, know that you are not alone and that each step, however small, is worthy of respect.

Reflection Prompt

What messages about authenticity did you receive from family, culture, or community?

Which ones have supported you, and which have held you back?

What new stories might you be ready to write for yourself?

SELF-COMPASSION: THE GROUND FOR NEW GROWTH

In a world that measures worth by achievement and appearance, the simple act of being kind to yourself is radical. Self-compassion is not self-indulgence; it is the ground from which true authenticity grows.

When you treat yourself gently, especially in moments of doubt, regret, or failure, you send a signal to your nervous system: I am safe, I am valued, I belong. From this place, you can risk more, try again, and offer the same compassion to others. Each time you choose kindness over criticism, you are quietly tending the soil for new growth within yourself.

Research shows that self-compassion increases resilience, motivation, and overall well-being. It softens the harshness of the inner critic and gives you the courage to return to yourself, even when you feel lost or unworthy. Self-compassion is both the starting place and the soft landing for your spiral home.

Try This

When you notice self-criticism, pause. Place a hand on your heart, cheek, or anywhere you feel comfort. Breathe gently. Say, "This is hard, and I am learning. May I meet myself with kindness right now." Notice what happens, immediately and over time.

If it feels awkward at first, that's normal. Let this practice be a quiet experiment, a way of offering yourself the same understanding you so freely give to others.

AUTHENTICITY AND RELATIONSHIPS: INVITATIONS TO REAL CONNECTION

Your authenticity is never just for you. Each time you bring more of your true self into a relationship by expressing a need, setting a boundary, or admitting vulnerability, you create the possibility for genuine connection.

This kind of honesty is not always easy, nor is it always welcomed. Some relationships will resist your growth. Some will change, some may end, and some will deepen in ways you could not have imagined. The risk is real, and so is the reward.

I have witnessed clients, students, and friends experience both loss and liberation as they grew into themselves. James found greater intimacy in his marriage by naming his struggles with anxiety. Erin discovered new energy and joy by finally claiming space for herself. Ana learned to disagree respectfully with classmates and became a more confident leader.

These stories are not about perfection. They are about practice, patience, and the willingness to choose self-respect over self-betrayal, even when the world or those closest to you may not always understand. Each act of authenticity, no matter how small, is an invitation, for yourself and for others, to step closer to what is real.

Journal Prompt

Is there a relationship where you long to be more real?

What would you risk and what might you gain by showing up as yourself, even a little more than before?

WHEN AUTHENTICITY MEETS ADVERSITY

The path of authenticity is not always one of triumph. Sometimes you will face loss, misunderstanding, or pain. You may encounter old wounds––shame, fear, the memory of rejection. Some days, survival is accomplishment enough. On those days, simply showing up as you are is an act of quiet courage.

In my work as a professor, I have seen students struggle with authenticity in the face of trauma, cultural pressure, or systemic barriers. Some rise, some falter, some retreat and then return again. Each journey, with all its twists and pauses, is worthy of honor.

Emerson's invitation is not to perform your "best self" for the world but to keep returning to what is most true for you, especially in adversity. When you can meet yourself with honesty and compassion, even when you are not "winning," you are practicing the greatest accomplishment of all. Every spiral back to self, no matter how slow or uncertain, is part of the journey.

AUTHENTICITY AS A SEED FOR SOCIAL CHANGE

It's easy to think of authenticity as a purely private affair, but in truth, every act of self-honoring is a seed for wider transformation. When you claim your own voice, you create space for others to do the same. Your willingness to be real is both an invitation and a challenge to your community, your profession, your world.

Our world desperately needs more people who are willing to be themselves, not as an act of rebellion but as a living commitment to integrity, justice, and love. The changes we seek, the healing we long for, all begin with the choice to show up as we are.

In my own life and work, I have witnessed the ripple effect of authenticity. Students who speak up in class inspire others to take risks. Leaders who own their mistakes create cultures of learning. Friends who dare to be honest invite deeper connection.

Reflection Prompt

Imagine the ripple effect your authenticity could have in your circles.

What small act of truth-telling might plant a seed of change for someone else?

PRACTICAL PRACTICES FOR AUTHENTIC LIVING

Morning inquiry

Each morning, pause and ask yourself, "How can I honor my truth today?" Write your answer, even if it feels small, incomplete, or uncertain. Let this question gently set the tone for your day.

Evening reflection

At day's end, notice when you were true to yourself and when you weren't. Celebrate the returns and forgive the detours. Each moment of return is a quiet victory on your spiral.

Body check-ins

Tune into your body. Notice where you feel most yourself, whether it's a feeling of ease, lightness, or groundedness. Stand, move, or breathe in ways that reconnect you to this center.

Permission slips

Write yourself a literal permission slip: "Today, I give myself permission to _____."

Use this tangible reminder as often as you need to give yourself grace and space.

Artistic expression

Paint, draw, dance, sing, or play. Creative acts often reveal truths that words cannot. Let your art be a doorway back to your authentic self.

Gentle challenges

Once a week, choose one area where you feel stuck or off balance. Ask yourself, "What would authenticity look like here?" Then experiment kindly and without pressure, letting curiosity guide you.

EMBRACING THE SHADOW: WHEN IT'S HARD TO BE YOURSELF

There will be times when authenticity feels too risky, too vulnerable, or too exhausting. This is normal. The shadow side of self-expression is often the longing for safety, acceptance, or simply rest. Old habits--people-pleasing, perfectionism, hiding--may return, sometimes uninvited.

Instead of shaming yourself for these moments, greet them with curiosity. What are these patterns protecting? What old fears or beliefs are asking for your attention? You can be gentle with these parts even as you practice new ways of being.

Try This

Write a letter to the part of yourself that wants to hide. Thank it for its service, for the protection it has offered. Ask what it needs to feel a little safer as you grow.

RETURNING, AGAIN AND AGAIN

To be yourself in a world that is constantly trying to make you something else is not a one-time achievement. It is a journey, a rhythm, a living spiral. You will forget, you will remember, you will drift and return. Each time you come home to yourself, you reinforce the foundation of a life aligned.

Remember, your journal is a faithful companion on this path, a place to experiment, to witness, and to welcome all parts of you, in every season.

Intention for these times:

Today, I honor my own nature.

When the world pushes, I pause and return to my center.

My truth is enough.

My journey is worthy.

To be myself, right here and right now, is a revolution.

FINAL REFLECTION

Set a timer for fifteen minutes and answer this question: "What does authenticity mean to me, today, in this season, with these challenges and gifts?"

Let your words be honest, imperfect, and unfiltered. Read them aloud. Notice how it feels to name your truth, knowing always that this act is both a beginning and an arrival.

Authenticity is the fertile ground from which all new vision grows. As you honor your own nature, you prepare yourself for the next step: imagining and claiming your unique vision for what is possible. As Emerson and your own heart remind you, the world may try to shape you, but your greatest accomplishment is to become yourself, again and again.

Let's now move into the art and practice of vision.

5. VISION: STEP 1 OF
THE 5-POINT PROCESS

Your vision will become clear only when you look into your heart. Who looks outside, dreams; who looks inside, awakes.

— CARL JUNG

LOOKING INWARD: VISION AS THE GATEWAY TO AWAKENING

IF YOU'RE HERE, you've already heard a call, a gentle nudge inviting you to awaken to something more than merely surviving the world's demands. This chapter is where we cross the threshold from intention into vision, the next turn of your spiral journey inward. The world outside, with its noise and endless invitations to become someone else, is not the source of your transformation. Your vision begins in the silence within, in the questions that echo softly, sometimes for years. Perhaps you sense a longing you can't quite name or a persistent discomfort that whispers you're meant for more. Here, Jung offers a radical permission: Look inside and trust that awakening is possible.

Vision is the birthplace of transformation, the spark that sets your inner landscape alight with purpose, direction, and possibility. Without vision, we do more than drift: we become numb, lost in obligations, caught in a culture that values conformity over awakening. We shrink into roles handed to us, react to the crises of others, or fill our days with busywork that quiets the deeper ache. But vision, even if just a flicker, a half-formed idea, or a stubborn whisper in the night, changes everything. With vision, you move from reacting to authoring, from adapting to creating. You begin to choose the life waiting to emerge from within––step by step, breath by breath.

Vision is not a linear plan. It's not a spreadsheet, a bucket list, or a polished manifesto for public consumption, though they all might come later. Vision is a pulse, a knowing that wells up from deep within. It is the ache that says, "This isn't all there is," and the sacred suspicion that you were meant for more.

Sometimes vision arrives as a clear call. More often it comes as an unanswered question, a sense of possibility, or a gentle pressure that refuses to be ignored. And, sometimes, it is a longing to awaken, to spiral deeper beyond the surface and touch what is real, what is yours.

Invitation

As you read, notice what arises inside you. Do you sense a flicker of more, a hunger to wake from the dream the world has handed you? Let yourself be gently curious. The beginning of all vision is permission to look inward and believe that what you find is trustworthy, even when the world outside tries to convince you otherwise.

VISION IS A LIVING RELATIONSHIP

Think back to the turning points of your own life. Were they products of a step-by-step plan? Or did they begin with a feeling, a flicker of hope, a vision, a question that wouldn't let go? Vision is what gives meaning to what you do not yet know. It is the light that shines through the cracks when your old stories fall apart.

Sometimes, vision whispers: "What if you could …?" Sometimes it arrives with a sense of dissatisfaction: "There must be more than this." Sometimes it emerges as a longing for wholeness, a call that pulls you forward even when you don't know where the path leads. These moments, whether subtle or seismic, can be exhilarating but also disorienting. Vision invites you to trust what you sense, even when you cannot explain it. It asks you to step out of old habits, carrying nothing but your inner wisdom for company.

Vision is not a one-time declaration. It is a living relationship, an ever-evolving spiral that grows, contracts, and transforms with you. Vision will sometimes challenge you, sometimes comfort you, and sometimes even break your heart. But when honored, it heals, it remakes, and it draws you into an ever-deepening connection with your own truth.

You do not need your vision to be fully formed to begin. Often, the very act of beginning is what clarifies and strengthens your vision. Treat it as a beloved companion, one whose presence you spiral back to again and again, especially when the world feels uncertain.

Reflect

As you read these words, you might pause for a moment and ask: When you think of vision, what images, sensations, or questions arise in you? You might allow yourself to linger here, without needing clarity. This is the beginning of your journey inward, where vision awakens.

VISION AND THE MESSY MIDDLE: PERMISSION TO NOT KNOW

Vision is rarely neat. It seldom arrives as a perfect, polished answer or a clear roadmap. More often, it unfolds slowly, shaped by trial, error, and uncertainty. Perhaps if you find yourself in the messy middle, feeling lost, uncertain, or "behind," know that you are not alone. This is evidence that you are alive, paying attention, and open to being transformed by what you discover.

Whether you're building a new life, forging a relationship, or launching a new venture, the creative process is almost always messy before it becomes meaningful. The old maps no longer fit the territory you're crossing now. The willingness to sit with discomfort, to ask honest questions, and to say "I don't know" is itself a sign of a waking life. It is here, in the fertile space of uncertainty, that vision grows strongest, but only if you are gentle and patient with yourself.

Imagine the spiral as it moves, sometimes sweeping wide, sometimes curling tight around the unknown. The messy middle is a natural turn in the spiral, a threshold where clarity hasn't yet arrived but transformation is quietly taking root.

Reflection Prompt

Perhaps you will notice one question you are living right now. You might write about it, letting yourself be honest, even if all you can say is, "I don't know, but I want to know." Allow yourself to notice how the very act of asking, the willingness to stay present in not-knowing, becomes the fertile ground for something new to emerge.

WHAT VISION REALLY IS (AND ISN'T)

Vision is your inner compass, a spiral turning within, not an external demand. In the noisy world outside, it's easy to confuse vision with pressure, believing you must be lost if you can't see every step ahead. But true vision is less about having a perfect map and more about sensing an inner resonance––a gentle yes, a quiet ping––that persists beneath the static of everyday life. It is both listening and dreaming, held in balance.

Vision is Courageous

Many of us have been taught to suppress our visions out of practicality, safety, or because we've learned that our deepest longings are unwelcome. The act of letting yourself want, of giving space to your desire even when you don't yet know what to do with it, is a radical act. Vision says, "I am worthy of wanting. I am willing to awaken."

Vision Is Not Fantasy

Fantasy stays in the head. Vision is felt deeply––in your body, in your very bones. Sometimes it's a quiet hope. Other times it arrives as envy or a physical sensation: a flutter, a tightness, an unmistakable ping. Vision calls for discernment. Is this longing a passing fancy or is it something deeper, something that endures and grows?

Vision Is Not a Privilege for the Few

It's easy to believe vision is reserved for those with resources or support. But some of the most powerful visions I've witnessed come from those who are struggling financially, emotionally, or socially. Vision is a birthright. It is sometimes the very thing that keeps us alive when nothing else makes sense.

Vision Is Not the Answer to Everything

Even the clearest vision doesn't guarantee the road will be easy or clear. You may feel more questions than answers, more longing than certainty. But vision offers you a place to return to, a spiral home inside yourself, a touchstone that helps you remember what matters when you are lost.

Prompt

Think of a time you felt a faint or persistent longing, even before you could name it.

Did you allow yourself to listen?

What happened when you ignored it?

What happened when you honored it, even a little?

WHY VISION IS HARD (AND WHY IT'S NEEDED NOW MORE THAN EVER)

We are living in a world noisy with other people's dreams, a swirling spiral of voices pulling us every which way. The dominant culture constantly tells us what is valuable, what we should want, and who we should become. Families hand down their scripts, sometimes out of love, sometimes out of fear. The media floods us with images and stories that blur the line between our own desires and someone else's fantasy. Even our closest friends may, with the best intentions, project their longings onto us.

I know this intimately. My mother, for example, often shares her hopes for me: a partner, a certain home, a particular rhythm of life. She means well, but there is a subtle invitation, sometimes a demand, to live her vision rather than mine. The pressure to conform, even when wrapped in love, is powerful. The world rewards us for fitting in, for adopting the goals and roles that keep things smooth.

Now add to this the wider upheaval: political, environmental, social, and it becomes clear why so many of us have learned to mute our visions. For those whose daily reality is survival, dreaming may feel impossible, even dangerous. Yet for others, uncertainty awakens a deeper need to reach for what truly matters. Sometimes, simply envisioning a future that is more just, more joyful, more awake becomes the most revolutionary act possible.

Everything in the status quo benefits from your resignation, your numbness, your settling for less. It takes courage, sometimes all the courage you have, to vision in a way that is true to your own soul. Jung's wisdom offers this: When you look within, you awaken not only for yourself but also become part of a much larger spiral of awakening that stretches to your community, your ancestors, and the generations yet to come.

When was the last time you let yourself imagine a future unfiltered by others' expectations? Take a moment now to write about it. What emerges when you give yourself full permission to vision without apology or restraint?

THE SCIENCE OF VISION: HOW THE BRAIN CREATES THE FUTURE

Neuroscience has begun to confirm what ancient wisdom traditions, artists, and mystics have always known: Vision is generative. The act of attending to a possibility, especially with feeling, primes your brain and your entire being to begin moving in that direction. Envisioning is not just positive thinking, it is a creative partnership with your biology.

The reticular activating system, a network in your brainstem, acts as a filter, letting in information that matches what you are seeking or expecting. It's why, after you get a new car or a particular gadget, you suddenly start seeing it everywhere. The mind notices what the heart is seeking.

This is also why visioning, using imagination, visualization, or guided imagery, can change not just your thoughts but your entire experience of possibility. Studies show that those who clarify and revisit their vision are significantly more likely to experience meaningful transformation, both in their actions and in their well-being.

When you imagine yourself living into your vision, your brain fires as if you are already taking those steps. Your body feels hope, excitement, sometimes even anxiety, your future self rehearsing reality. This isn't magic, but it is magical: The more vividly and often you engage with your vision, the more you create a future memory, guiding your choices and opening doors that might otherwise stay closed.

Exercise

Find a quiet place and, with soft eyes or closed, allow yourself five gentle minutes. Sit comfortably and imagine a scene from your life where you are living your vision. What do you see? How does your body feel? What details emerge, maybe colors, sounds, even smells?

Afterwards, write in your journal: What surprised you? What felt awkward, and what felt awakening?

ADVANCED NEUROSCIENCE OF VISION: THE EMBODIED FUTURE

Let's go even deeper. Vision is not just a thought in the mind, it is embodied. Research into neuroplasticity reveals that vividly imagining yourself living your vision strengthens neural circuits, making change more possible. Dr. Joe Dispenza and others have shown that when you rehearse the future, your brain and body begin to behave as if the new reality is already here. This doesn't mean that wishing alone will bring results, but your entire system becomes more ready, more creative, more resilient.

Pairing vision with emotion is powerful. The more you allow yourself to feel the yes of your vision, hope, excitement, even healthy nervousness, the more you prime your mind to notice, risk, and move toward what matters. Each time you act as if your vision is true, you reinforce the pathways that make it so.

Practice

Try embodied visioning each morning for a week. Before you begin your day, take a breath and invite your body to express, even subtly, how it would feel to live your vision. Stand, move, stretch, breathe as your future self would.

Afterward, jot a few notes in your journal. Notice: Does your day unfold differently? Do new insights or opportunities arise?

VISION, DIVERSITY, AND THE COLLECTIVE FUTURE

Pause for a moment and think about those whose visions have shifted entire worlds. Dr. Martin Luther King Jr. stood at the crossroads of brutality and hope, declaring a vision that became a blueprint for justice, dignity, and what he called the "beloved community." Frida Kahlo transformed pain into paint, longing into image, refusing to be erased or defined by anyone else's expectations. Maya Angelou found the courage to sing her truth into the world's deaf places. And Georgia O'Keeffe, a presence close to my own heart and history, shaped her vision among the wild, sun-bleached bones and vast skies of New Mexico, making a home in the desert and capturing its mystery with uncompromising clarity.

What unites these visionaries is not certainty, privilege, or ease but a willingness to awaken to a longing deeper than fear and to risk sharing it, boldly and tenderly. Their visions were not safe, comfortable, or universally understood. Many paid dearly for their boldness, yet their willingness to look within, rather than only outside, created ripples that changed not only their own lives but the lives of countless others. Their legacies offer living proof that sometimes the most radical act we can undertake is simply to hold a vision in a world that is often content with resignation.

Visioning is often an act of survival and defiance for those whose identities, dreams, or truths exist at the margins, whose voices have been muted or dismissed. In such contexts, even the act of imagining safety, dignity, or joy is revolutionary. When you declare, "I am willing to reach for the feast my soul was born for," you step into a lineage of ancestors, some known, many forgotten, who dared to awaken and risk more. This, too, is what Jung meant by looking within: awakening not only for self but for others, for now, and for the generations to come.

Your vision is both deeply personal and inherently collective. It carries echoes of ancestral courage and hope. It ripples outward, touching those you may never meet but whose lives shift because you chose to stand in your truth.

Prompt

What part of your vision feels connected to something or someone bigger than yourself?

Does your longing carry an ancestral echo?

How does your vision ripple outward?

Let yourself write, draw, or simply notice what arises. There are many ways to honor the stirring of what wants to be born.

HOW VISION IS NURTURED AND PROTECTED

Vision, especially in its earliest stages, is delicate. It rarely grows in isolation. In my work, I see again and again how even a single witness like a friend, mentor, therapist, or group, can transform a fragile hope into a living possibility. Sometimes, vision is less born and more "midwifed" by those who listen deeply, hold space tenderly, and offer gentle permission.

For some, vision is a thread woven through generations. You may carry dreams that your ancestors could not claim: a longing for freedom, for love, for creative expression. In honoring your vision, you become part of a healing lineage, quietly saying, "The story does not end with me." For others, vision arises from a sense of calling, spirit, or guidance, an invitation from beyond your own experience to participate in something larger than yourself.

You may find it helpful to use ritual, journaling, creative play, or community to protect and nurture your vision as it takes root. Vision boards, writing, meditation, prayer, or even daydreaming can make vision more tangible. Don't hesitate to experiment with what feels real and alive to you.

It's important to be discerning in the early stages. Not everyone will understand your vision, and some may respond from their own fears or disappointments. Be gentle with yourself. Share your vision only with those who nurture it, allowing it to gather strength before exposing it to doubt or criticism. Think of your vision as a seedling: precious, growing, needing sunlight and safe space.

Journal Prompt

Who do you trust to share your vision with?

Where do you feel safe to let your dream breathe, even if it remains fragile?

Where might you need boundaries or new community to help your vision grow?

Linger with what arises.

VISION TROUBLESHOOTING: WHAT IF I CAN'T SEE MY VISION?

It's not uncommon to feel blocked, lost, or frustrated when you try to clarify your vision. Sometimes vision slips underground for a season, retreating quietly beneath the surface. Other times it is obscured by old stories, fear, grief, or even exhaustion. If you're stuck, you might find yourself considering these gentle invitations, whispers from your own inner guide to help you step closer to what wants to emerge.

Release Perfectionism

Your vision does not have to be grand, noble, or even fully formed to matter. Start wherever you are: "I want more ease." "I want to laugh more." "I long for deeper connection." Even the smallest longing is worthy. Sometimes a tiny spark is all that's needed to light a new path.

Attend to Your Body

When the mind is noisy or overwhelmed, drop into your body. Where do you feel curiosity or excitement? What gives you a sense of *ping* versus *thud*? Sometimes, simply noticing what enlivens you, whether a flutter of hope or a gentle pull, is enough to begin moving toward your vision.

Follow the Green-Eyed Monster

Envy, surprisingly, can be a powerful compass. Who or what sparks envy in you? Instead of shaming yourself, get curious: What desire is being mirrored? Often, this is your vision waving to you from across the room, inviting you to claim it as your own.

Get Playful

If there were no rules, what would you try? What's your secret "If only ..." dream? Play frees the inner visionary who's been waiting for permission to step forward. Allow yourself to dream with lightness and curiosity.

Honor the Not Knowing

Vision can also be an inquiry, a spiral of questions: "What am I longing for?" "What would I love to explore?" "What haven't I dared to want?" Let these questions spiral gently through your mind, opening doors and inviting new paths rather than demanding answers.

Exercise

Write a letter to yourself from the future you who has trusted their vision. What comfort or wisdom do they offer? What surprises have unfolded on the journey? Allow yourself to listen deeply as you write, as if this future self is speaking directly to your heart.

WHEN VISION COLLIDES WITH REALITY

Vision is beautiful, but it can also be disruptive. When you begin to see clearly what you truly want, the distance between your current life and your emerging truth can feel startling. This awareness may stir grief, anger, impatience, or frustration. You may suddenly recognize that a job, a relationship, or even your daily routines are no longer aligned with what your deeper self is calling for. These moments can be painful to acknowledge, yet they are also the fertile ground where real change begins.

It is natural to feel resistance, fear, or even resentment when vision reveals these gaps. Instead of pushing these feelings away or judging them as signs of failure, try meeting them with curiosity. You might gently ask yourself:

What is my discomfort trying to teach me?

What small step could I take right now to honor my vision, even if imperfectly?

Sometimes the first step toward transformation is simply to grieve what has not worked, to allow yourself to feel the loss of old dreams or familiar patterns. Your journal, your rituals, and your body can be safe places to witness and honor this tender process. You may need to slow down, seek support, or make room for uncertainty. Trust that even when everything feels messy or unfinished, the awakening has already begun to take shape within you.

Prompt

Write a letter to your current self from the version of you who has honored your vision. What comfort, reassurance, or new perspective does that future self offer? What would they want you to remember on the days when the gap between vision and reality feels wide and daunting?

VISION IN PRACTICE

Vision does not need to be grand or dramatic. It can be as simple as a quiet longing for deeper connection, for work that feels meaningful, or for a sense of belonging. Sometimes, vision is born in moments of stillness: watching the sunrise, sitting in meditation, or hearing a line of poetry that pierces your heart.

Practice: The Vision Scan

Settle into a quiet space. With your eyes closed or softly open, scan your life for any area that feels heavy, stuck, or lifeless. What would you love to feel or experience there instead? Allow images, words, and sensations to arise naturally. Without judging, write down whatever comes, no matter how modest, surprising, or wild.

Then, gently ask yourself:

Where do I feel the faintest ping?

Where is there a spark, however small?

If I could whisper one hope to myself for the coming year, what would it be?

Allow this practice to be a gentle exploration, a quiet spiral inward that invites your vision to take shape in its own time and way.

THE ROLE OF IMAGINATION AND PLAY

Visioning can feel heavy if we treat it only as serious work. But remember, some of the most powerful visions arise in moments of play, creativity, or unstructured time. Allow yourself the freedom to doodle, sing, collage, or move your body as you imagine new possibilities. These playful acts open doors that logic alone cannot unlock.

Sometimes, childlike play is the key to bypassing the inner critic and inviting deeper wisdom to surface. Don't be afraid to daydream. Make space for laughter, wonder, and experimentation. Vision doesn't have to look productive or serious to be powerful. In fact, it often works best when it's light, joyful, and free.

Prompt

If you could play at visioning, what would you try? What feels most fun or freeing right now?

Let your imagination take the lead. Notice what arises when you let go of expectations and simply play.

THE DOLPHIN WELCOME AND THE MOVE TO MÉXICO

There are moments in life when your vision becomes unmistakably real, not just an inner yearning but a lived experience that changes you forever. I remember so vividly standing at the edge of change some years ago, my heart alive with the possibility of a move from New Mexico to Florida. The vision for my new life was so clear it nearly vibrated: a place of renewal, a sense of home, a chance to live in resonance with something I had longed for. But, as is often the case, the path was not simple. The logistics thudded heavily in my mind: How would I afford the move? What would I do about my beloved pets, my dog and two cats, who were family to me? Each challenge felt like a test of my commitment to the vision that called.

A wise teacher once asked me, "Does this choice ping or thud?" I found myself returning to that question with each decision. The ping of possibility was undeniable, but so too were the thuds of resistance. Yet vision does not require the absence of obstacles; it only asks for your willingness to move forward, even as you work through what stands in the way. This is what Jung meant by awakening: It is not a one-time event but instead a practice of honoring what is real inside you, even as the world outside challenges your resolve.

As I surrendered the need to control every outcome, the universe responded in kind. The right home appeared for my pets through a single, serendipitous call. Financial support arrived when I needed it most. My job shifted in ways that freed me to move, and a beautiful living space emerged, almost as if by magic. Looking back, it felt orchestrated by a force much larger than myself.

That first night in Florida, after a long journey, I walked out onto a dock with two friends. The moon was bright and the air electric with newness. Suddenly, we heard a splash––three dolphins playing in the water below. They surfaced, circled, and then disappeared into the night. In that moment, I felt a deep, wordless knowing: My vision had not only guided me but had conspired with life to welcome me home. That dolphin encounter was more than a sign, it was a reflection of everything I had learned about honoring the pings, trusting the process, and letting my inner vision lead, even when the way was uncertain.

Years later, when I was called to México, I recognized the same energetic signature: a *yes* that hummed through my being, paired with a familiar parade of thuds: uncertainty, loss, and the unfamiliar. This time, the vision included living alone in a new land, learning a new language, and building community from the ground up. There were practical challenges–– rehoming a saltwater aquarium, letting go of Lola the cat, and saying goodbye to a version of myself that had grown comfortable. Still, the magic returned: Support came from unexpected places, new friends emerged, and the universe sent small but unmistakable signs that I was on the right path.

Each move taught me that vision is not a single leap but a series of choices, a willingness to listen, to trust, to follow the faintest inner ping, and to allow the world to meet you halfway. It is in these moments, when vision moves from the inside out and the world conspires in your favor, that awakening becomes real, embodied, and truly your own.

WRESTLING WITH VISION

Miguel's Quiet Yes

Miguel came to me at a crossroads, uncertain about leaving a secure job for a path that felt truer but far less certain. As a first-generation college student from a close-knit Mexican American family, he carried the hopes and worries of his loved ones alongside his own. His vision was clear, a life in counseling, a chance to serve his community, especially young men and boys who rarely spoke of their pain. Yet each step forward met resistance: family doubts, financial anxiety, the weight of being the first to walk a new road. He described his vision as a "ping so strong I feel it in my chest," but said everything around it felt impossible.

Together, we worked to separate the energy of vision from the noise of resistance. What did that ping feel like in his body? Where did he sense excitement or fear? Over time, Miguel learned to honor the ping, even in small ways, attending an informational session, sharing his dream with his parents, seeking out scholarships. Each action was an act of faith, a willingness to move even when the path felt incomplete. And, as often happens when vision is honored, life responded: A mentor appeared, financial support arrived, and a neighbor's story echoed Miguel's dream. Miguel's journey was not a straight line, but each small step deepened his awakening, and the magic he experienced reinforced his trust in the process.

Jade's Unfolding Dream

Jade had always straddled the worlds of art and healing. For years, they were told to choose—one path, one story, one identity. But their true vision was plural: to build a healing arts collective for BIPOC and queer voices who felt left out of mainstream wellness spaces. For Jade, vision arrived as flashes, images, colors, moments of certainty, but each was met by waves of doubt, skepticism from friends, and the weight of "Who am I to do this?" We practiced tuning into the difference between other people's opinions and their own inner compass.

For Jade, the work of vision was both practical and spiritual: applying for grants, learning about business, letting go of friendships that couldn't travel this new path, and finding joy in the company of those who celebrated their full self. As their collective slowly came to life, Jade was continually surprised by synchronicity, a co-founder showing up "by accident," an old teacher reappearing as a guide, the first open house filled with laughter and possibility. Their unfolding story became a testament to the power of honoring vision. Even, and especially, when it defies easy explanation.

THE VISION BOARD REIMAGINED

Vision boards are just one way to honor what calls to you. For some, the process of cutting, pasting, and arranging images on traditional vision boards becomes a powerful ritual, making vision visible and real. For others, vision boards have evolved into digital collages that shift and grow with you, folders of photographs that evoke longing and joy, playlists that hold the energy of a dream.

What matters most is not the form but the act of giving your vision a home outside your mind, a tangible place to return to.

Clients have shared wildly creative approaches, journaling vision letters to their future selves, creating altars with meaningful objects, even drawing maps of places they wish to visit or inhabit within themselves. The point is not perfection but participation: making your vision visible in a way that feels alive and true for you.

Sometimes, what begins as a vision board becomes an evolving art project, a living prayer, or simply a quiet reminder that your longing is real and worthy of attention.

Prompt

How might you give your vision a physical or creative home? What medium––art, music, movement, storytelling––feels most natural for you? Try giving your vision form and notice what shifts in your body, your energy, and your willingness to awaken to new possibilities.

THE SEASONS OF VISION: HONORING THE CYCLES

Vision, like everything alive, moves in cycles. It flows through seasons, times of vivid clarity and urgency, like the first green shoots of spring or the radiant exuberance of summer. In these moments, your vision bursts forth, calling you to act, to dream boldly, to step into new possibilities with fresh energy.

Yet there are other times when vision feels quiet, dormant beneath the surface, an underground seed gathering strength in the stillness, a gentle longing that hasn't yet found its words. Sometimes you are called to plant, to nurture tender shoots, to harvest the fruits of your labor, or simply to rest and renew. Each season holds its own sacred purpose, none permanent, all necessary.

It's natural, and essential, for vision to shift as you grow. What once electrified you may become less relevant as you enter a new phase of life. Allow yourself to honor the vision that has served you, to grieve its passing with compassion, and to create space for new possibilities to emerge without judgment. Trust that every cycle is an invitation to deepen your awakening, your insight, and your relationship with yourself.

The spiral of vision is not about rushing forward but about dancing with these rhythms, leaning into what each season offers, even when it feels slow or uncertain. In this dance, you discover the wisdom of timing, the grace of patience, and the resilience that comes from honoring your own pace.

Journal Reflection

Notice which season of vision you are in right now. What seeds are you planting? Allow yourself to see what you are tending to as a growing vision. Are you harvesting fruits from your efforts, or are you resting and renewing for what's next? You might find yourself musing about what honors you this season while you welcome its lessons with openness.

WHEN VISION CHANGES: THE ART OF LETTING GO

Sometimes, the hardest part of visioning is letting go: of an old dream, a former identity, or a life that no longer fits. Vision is not a contract signed in permanence with your past self but a living, evolving relationship. There will be moments when the vision you carried with such passion has given you all it could. Letting it go is not failure; it is a sign of wisdom, of growth, and of the courage to remain awake and present to what's next.

To outgrow a vision can bring relief, grief, or even confusion. Allow yourself to honor what your old dreams gave you, the lessons learned, the growth achieved, the meaning experienced. Then, gently ask: What wants to emerge now? By making space for what is new, you align with the deepest kind of authenticity, an ongoing awakening to your life as it is, and as it is becoming.

Prompt

Write about a dream or vision you have outgrown. What did it give you?

What new longing or possibility is now asking for your attention?

TENDING THE FLAME: RETURNING TO VISION

Vision is not a one-time event but a practice, a spiral that brings you back to the heart of what matters, again and again. As life changes, so will your vision. Sometimes it will expand, sometimes it will shrink, and sometimes it will disappear and reappear in surprising forms. This ebb and flow is normal, wise, and worthy of celebration.

I encourage you to keep a dedicated space in your journal, a place for vision updates. Here, you can record what currently pings for you, what questions or doubts arise, and what dreams refuse to fade. Over months and years, this living archive becomes a map, not of linear progress but of your evolving relationship with possibility and awakening.

Prompt

Write a letter to your future self, describing the life you imagine a year from now if you were to trust your vision fully. Let the letter be detailed, loving, and honest. When you read it back, notice what surprises, excites, or unsettles you. This, too, is part of the spiral of awakening.

MEETING RESISTANCE: THE THUDS ALONG THE WAY

Every vision, no matter how bright or compelling, will meet resistance. Doubt may creep in. Fear may whisper. Practical obstacles may appear, sometimes suddenly, sometimes persistently. When these thuds arise, do not see them as signs that you are failing or off course. Instead, welcome them as companions on the journey of awakening, markers that signal you are pushing toward something real and meaningful.

Each thud is an invitation to pause, to lean in with curiosity rather than judgment. You might ask yourself gently:

What is this resistance trying to teach me?

What support might I need right now?

What small, imperfect action could help me move forward despite the obstacles?

Resistance is not your enemy but instead a necessary rhythm in the dance of visioning. It shapes your growth and strengthens your resolve. Like a wave that momentarily pushes you back before carrying you forward, resistance can be the catalyst that makes your commitment clearer, your steps more deliberate, your heart more courageous.

Exercise

Take a moment to list every thud you feel as you work with your vision, all the doubts, the fears, the setbacks, the moments you want to give up. Next to each, write down one small action you could take or someone you could ask for support. This might be as simple as taking a deep breath, sending a message to a friend, or stepping away for a moment of rest.

Remind yourself often: Courage is not the absence of resistance but the willingness to act anyway, however imperfectly. Each step you take, even in the face of a thud, is a quiet victory on your spiral of awakening.

VISION AND THE 5-POINT PROCESS

Vision is first among the 5 Points for a very good reason. It is the beacon that calls you forward, the why that breathes life into every other step: Commitment, Awareness, Living Into, and Integration. Vision is not only your inspiration; it is your guiding star when you feel lost, your fuel in moments when the path is steep or unclear.

Without vision, the steps that follow risk becoming directionless, mechanical, or hollow. But with vision, every other point becomes a way to give form, color, and expression to the possibility that has awakened within you. It is the living thread that weaves the whole process together, turning abstract hopes into palpable reality.

Yet vision alone is not enough. A beautiful vision, no matter how compelling, can fade if it remains just a dream, if it is not paired with commitment, daily practice, and the ongoing work of integrating your awakening into the very fabric of your life. Vision must be nurtured and embodied to move from idea to lived truth.

In the chapters to come, you will be gently guided in moving from vision to embodiment, from dreaming to living. You will learn how to step forward, spiral by spiral, at your own pace and in your own way, honoring both the light and the shadows of this unfolding journey.

Let your vision be both your compass and your companion. Keep it close, and trust that it will guide you through the unknown, into a life aligned with your deepest self.

THE POWER OF COMMUNITY AND COLLECTIVE VISION

While your vision is uniquely yours, it does not exist in isolation. At our core, we are relational beings, wired for belonging and resonance. When your vision is shared, witnessed, or supported by even a single person, its energy is multiplied and protected. Community is not about numbers or crowds. It might be one friend, a trusted mentor, a small circle of like-minded seekers, or an online space where your vision can breathe, grow, and be met with encouragement rather than judgment.

Over the years, I've witnessed the magic that unfolds when visioning is done collectively. In small circles and workshops, I've seen participants hesitate to speak their deepest hopes, and then, after witnessing someone else's vulnerability, find the courage to share their own. It is as if each authentic vision grants permission for others to awaken too. This is the ripple effect of vision: Your willingness to honor your longing lights a path for others, especially those who are still searching for theirs.

If you feel called, seek out or create a space for shared visioning. This might be as formal as a mastermind group or as simple as a regular coffee with a friend who "gets it." Offer to witness and support each other's dreams. Celebrate progress, mourn setbacks together, and gently remind one another that the act of visioning is itself a powerful act of hope, resistance, and awakening.

Prompt

Who in your life has helped you hold a vision when you doubted yourself?

How might you invite more support or community into your visioning process?

If you feel the absence of such support, what step, however small, could you take to begin building it?

CLOSING INTEGRATION: VISION AS SACRED TRUST

Vision is not merely a first step on a checklist; it is an ongoing invitation to partnership, with yourself, with the world, and with what Jung called the Self, that deepest, most alive part of your being. Each time you honor your vision, you say yes to awakening. You choose not to settle for the outer world's script but to trust the inner wisdom that grows every time you look inside and truly listen.

As you move into the next phase, Commitment, remember that vision is both fragile and fierce. It will evolve, contract, and expand as you do. Keep returning to it, updating it, and allowing it to surprise you. Carry this trust with you: The life that wants to emerge from you is not random but deeply meaningful. Your vision is a sacred trust, a spiral weaving together your past, present, and the future you are quietly building.

Prompt

As you finish this chapter, complete this sentence:

"When I honor my vision, I ..."

Allow yourself to write freely, perhaps listing, rambling, or spiraling outward to expand what's already there. Write until you surprise yourself, until you glimpse something new, perhaps even something that brings a sense of awe or quiet joy.

A FINAL INVITATION: TRUSTING YOUR AWAKENING

If you take just one thing from this chapter, let it be this: The world outside may always be trying to make you something else. Your own mind may at times resist, doubt, or second-guess. But every time you return to the vision in your heart, you are choosing awakening over sleepwalking, freedom over resignation, and meaning over numbness.

The invitation now is to keep visioning, not as a once-and-done exercise but as a way of life. Trust that every longing, every question, every ping is a doorway. Trust that even when you cannot see the whole staircase, you are allowed to take the next step. And trust, above all, that the act of visioning, of looking inside, listening, and awakening, is not just a personal practice but a gift and offering to a world in need of new ways of seeing, new stories, and new hope.

As you move forward, your journal, your body, your imagination, and your community are your allies. Let them hold you, challenge you, and support you as you deepen this partnership with possibility.

Final Prompt for Chapter 5

Set aside ten or fifteen minutes and return to your journal. Begin with the sentence: "When I honor my vision, I ..."

Let yourself write, draw, sing, or dream as you need. Notice what arises in your body, your energy, your mood. When you finish, read your words aloud and listen deeply. Notice what colors, textures, or feelings emerge on the page. Is there something you've named here that you are ready to carry forward into commitment, the next step of this spiral journey?

Vision lights the path, but it is commitment that gives you the courage to walk it. As you clarify what's possible for your life, the next step is to choose, again and again, to keep moving forward, even when the way is uncertain.

Now, let's explore how commitment turns vision into lived reality.

6. COMMITMENT: STEP 2 OF THE 5-POINT PROCESS

The moment one definitely commits oneself, then Providence moves too.

— W.H. MURRAY

THE MYSTERY AND POWER OF COMMITMENT

IF YOU'RE READING THIS, you've already spent time visioning, feeling the stirrings of possibility in your life. Perhaps you've touched moments of deep clarity, a ping in your body, a whisper from your soul, a glimpse of a new reality. But there comes a point when vision alone, no matter how vivid, is not enough. The difference between a life that remains in the realm of longing and one that truly transforms is commitment. This step is the hinge, where dreams are quietly, yet irrevocably, turned into reality.

Commitment is more than a promise or a wish written in your journal. It's the moment your inner *yes* becomes an anchor, rooting you in a new story even when the winds pick up and the old world pulls at your sleeves. Commitment is what remains when inspiration wanes and difficulty arrives. It is the spiritual practice of saying, "I am in. I will return to this, again and again, until the new becomes the familiar."

W.H. Murray's words, like Jung's before him, invite you to consider something larger than effort alone. He reminds us that the act of committing oneself fully, not just with words but with heart and action, sets unseen forces in motion. Providence moves too. Life begins to organize itself around your devotion, meeting you in ways you couldn't have predicted from the starting line. Commitment, then, is not only a personal act but a cosmic invitation, a handshake with the unknown, a silent agreement with your own becoming.

Reflect

As you read, you might notice a subtle shift inside, a readiness, a quiver of fear, a surge of resistance or hope. All are welcome here. Commitment rarely arrives as a blaring trumpet. Instead, it is often quiet, a soft insistence that will not let you go. What is stirring in you right now, as you cross this threshold from dreaming to doing?

COMMITMENT IS NOT A FEELING

In a culture obsessed with inspiration, we often mistake commitment for an emotion, a rush of certainty, a flash of motivation that we imagine will carry us across every finish line. But commitment is deeper, quieter, and far steadier than any feeling. It is a vow made in the presence of both hope and doubt, a quiet promise whispered to yourself: Even on the days I don't feel it, I will return.

So many people wait for the "right feeling" before they begin. The perfect clarity, the absence of fear, the promise of ease. But life rarely offers these gifts at the outset. More often, commitment is the act of beginning anyway, of taking the first uncertain step even as your knees tremble. This is what Murray means: Providence waits for your signal. It does not move until you do.

Imagine a gardener planting seeds before the rain arrives, committing to the process before there's any visible reward. The act of planting is a promise made in faith that growth will come. In much the same way, your commitment signals to life that you are ready, even if your feelings waver.

The real magic of commitment is what unfolds after you say yes. Feelings will come and go, doubts may circle back, but commitment weaves a golden thread through every season, tying you to the deeper why behind your actions. In this way, you become both witness and participant in your own unfolding.

Invitation

You might pause for a moment and notice:

Where in your life have you been waiting for the perfect feeling before taking action?

What small, faithful step could you take now, planting your own seed of intention, trusting that the feelings will follow?

THE PARADOX: FREEDOM THROUGH DEVOTION

There is a paradox at the heart of commitment: It can seem like a limitation, yet it is where true freedom is born. When you say yes to one thing, be it a path, a relationship, a value, you are released from scattering your energy in a thousand directions. Suddenly, you are free to focus, to deepen, to build real intimacy with your life.

Without commitment, it's easy to drift from project to project or relationship to relationship, always hungry, never quite satisfied. Commitment is what allows love to take root, art to mature, communities to flourish. What you water grows. What you return to, again and again, becomes a living thing.

True commitment is less a battle with yourself and more a quiet surrender to what you already know, deep inside, that you want. Sometimes, all you need is permission to notice that a decision has already begun to blossom within you. When you make that inward promise, life itself begins to organize around your yes, helping you return, especially when you waver.

Prompt:Recall a time when you made a commitment that changed you. How did your life begin to organize itself around that yes?Were there moments you wavered, and if so, what helped you return?

THE ANATOMY OF COMMITMENT

Commitment is a living, breathing thing, a quiet force that shapes the contours of your days and determines what truly takes root in your life. Yet, commitment is so often misunderstood. Some imagine it's about willpower, a grim determination to push through no matter what. Others fear that making a commitment will chain them to something that may not fit tomorrow, as if saying yes now locks every door to freedom in the future.

The truth, though, is more nuanced, and more liberating. Commitment is about devotion, not rigidity. It is an ongoing dance between resolve and surrender, a willingness to return, to re-decide, to let your why evolve even as you stay the course. In the language of the 5-Point Process, commitment is the act of placing your vision on the altar of your life, day after day, even when you feel uninspired, afraid, or simply tired. It becomes the structure that holds you upright when storms come and the safe container that lets you risk growing.

When you truly commit, you make a pact, not only with yourself but with life itself. As Murray reminds us, something mysterious and alive begins to unfold only when you step forward with full intention. Unseen hands appear. Helpers cross your path. Doors open. Commitment is the key that unlocks the synchrony between your desire and what the world is willing to offer in return.

Core Qualities of Commitment

1. Willingness to Choose

Commitment starts with a choice. Not a forever, carved-in-stone declaration, but an honest *yes* in this moment. This yes may need to be renewed a thousand times. It is less about certainty and more about willingness to try, to risk, to be changed by what unfolds.

2. Resilience and Return

No commitment, no matter how authentic, is free from challenge. You will falter, forget, and question yourself. But commitment is measured by your willingness to return. In the spiral of transformation, every return is sacred, a living sign of devotion, not of failure.

3. **Flexibility and Self-Compassion**

Rigid commitment snaps under pressure. Living commitment is flexible, able to adapt and shift course when new information or circumstances arise. To stay truly committed is to be gentle with yourself, celebrating the wins, forgiving the setbacks, making space for change. The paradox is this: The more compassionate you are with yourself, the deeper and more sustainable your commitment will be.

4. **Daily Action**

Commitment lives in what you do, not just in what you say. Small repeated actions, such as journaling, mindful breathing, honest conversations, seeking support, become the bones and sinew of a committed life. Grand gestures may fade, but these small acts accumulate, each one another stitch in the tapestry of transformation.

Micropractice

Pause for a moment and bring your attention to your breath. Ask yourself softly: Where in my life do I feel the quiet pulse of commitment, however small?Let an image, memory, or recent act come to mind. Notice if it's accompanied by willingness, by return, by flexibility, by a single step repeated.

Now, gently affirm: I can renew my commitment in any moment. Each return is enough. Every small act is a seed.

Carry this awareness into the next part of your day, letting commitment be a living thread, gentle, flexible, and always available.

THE MYTHS OF COMMITMENT (AND HOW THEY KEEP US STUCK)

Commitment can feel daunting, not only because of what it asks but because of the stories we inherit about what it means. These myths keep us circling the edges, afraid to step in fully. Let's bring them into the light and see what's really true.

Myth 1: Commitment Means Giving Up Freedom

Many believe that commitment is a cage, a loss of possibility. In reality, commitment is what creates real freedom. Without it, we drift, battered by the winds of urgency and distraction, never quite finding rest. When you commit, you free yourself from the endless fatigue of indecision, and you discover the quiet joy of depth. Depth, not breadth, is where meaning and belonging are found. The roots that hold you steady also let you grow tall.

Myth 2: Commitment Requires Certainty

It's easy to imagine that commitment can only follow total clarity, that you must wait until you're 100 percent sure before you say yes. But this is a recipe for paralysis. Most meaningful commitments are made in the presence of uncertainty. You choose, you act, and in the doing, you learn what is true. The path clarifies only as you walk it, step by imperfect step.

Myth 3: Commitment Is a One-Time Decision

The fantasy is tempting: One grand yes, and you're set for life. In truth, every meaningful commitment is renewed, day after day, sometimes hour by hour. The power is not in the initial spark but in the willingness to return to it, especially after setbacks. Commitment is a living thing, not a relic.

Myth 4: Commitment Must Be All or Nothing

Our culture often insists on going all in or not at all. But sometimes, the wisest commitment is partial, gradual, a series of small yeses that gather strength over time. You may commit to showing up for five minutes, not five hours. You may give yourself to the practice as you are, not as you hope to be. This too is enough. The spiral widens with each return.

Myth 5: Commitment Means Never Wavering

To be human is to waver. Commitment is not about never questioning, it's about always coming back, like the tide returning to shore. The wobble is not a sign of failure but proof that you are alive, learning, and engaged. Every return is evidence of your devotion, not its absence.

Reflection

Which of these myths feels most familiar to you?

Where have they kept you circling the edge of a true yes?

How might it feel to let go of even one, to allow commitment to become a source of freedom, resilience, and gentle return?

THE SPIRAL OF COMMITMENT

Commitment is rarely a straight line; it is more like a spiral, with returns and departures, gentle circles that deepen over time. Real change lives in the willingness to come back, again and again, however imperfectly.

Sarah's Spiral

Sarah arrived certain she was "bad at commitment." Diets, exercise routines, self-help programs. She met each with a burst of enthusiasm that fizzled into guilt and self-blame. "I can't stick with anything," she told me. "I always end up quitting."

We began to explore what commitment could mean, if freed from the myth of all or nothing. We shifted from grand promises to gentle, daily returns. Rather than "I will work out every day forever," Sarah chose five minutes of movement, most days, with compassion for days she missed. She stopped punishing herself and started tracking her spiral, acknowledging that real change is never linear. Some days were easier, some harder, but each return counted.

Over time, her relationship with commitment softened and deepened. She began to notice that even after a week of falling off, she returned more quickly, with less shame. She realized her commitment wasn't measured by unbroken success but by her willingness to return, forgive, and try again. This, she saw, was what allowed her to actually grow, and, perhaps most beautifully, to love herself in the process.

David's Commitment to Healing

David, a retired engineer, came to me grieving the loss of his wife. He wanted a roadmap, something to "fix" the pain and bring wholeness. Instead, he committed to a simple daily practice: writing a letter to his wife or himself every morning, no matter how he felt.

There were days David resented the ritual. Sometimes he wrote only a single sentence. Sometimes he skipped writing entirely. But his commitment to the process, to show up imperfectly, to honor his pain, to be present with himself, became a lifeline. Over months, small shifts appeared: The letters grew longer, tears gave way to laughter, and moments of hope surfaced in the writing.

For David, commitment was not about fixing grief but about staying with the spiral of healing. The act of returning, again and again, became its own medicine, allowing healing to emerge on its own timeline.

Invitation

Where in your life have you mistaken commitment for perfection or a straight road?

What might shift if you allowed your commitment to be a spiral, a practice of returning, forgiving, and gently beginning again?

THE ROLE OF INTENTION IN COMMITMENT

Commitment never arises in a vacuum. It is always rooted in intention, a living, conscious *why* that nourishes you when the road gets rough. If vision is the invitation and intention the spark, commitment is the daily act of showing up, embodying your deepest why, even as your initial inspiration comes and goes.

You might imagine intention as the riverbed and commitment as the water, each shaping and being shaped by the other, day by day. Without intention, commitment can become hollow, a rigid rule, a stale routine, a promise with no heartbeat. But when your intention is alive, commitment becomes an act of devotion, a renewal of purpose in each breath, each step, each gentle return.

It's important to revisit your intention often, letting it grow with you. Ask yourself, Why am I committing to this, right now? Sometimes, intentions evolve, deepen, or change shape entirely. Stay curious. If your intention feels old, heavy, or lifeless, pause. Recommit only to what feels real and honest now. True commitment is flexible; it matures as you do.

Prompt

Take a quiet moment to write your current intention for this commitment. Let it be alive, specific, and true, something you can feel in your body, not just something that sounds good. Read it aloud to yourself and notice: Does your body lean in or pull away? Let your intention be a living thing, guiding your commitment forward.

COMMITMENT AS UNCONSCIOUS BUY-IN

One of the most powerful and mysterious aspects of commitment is the unconscious agreement that happens beneath the surface. You may consciously choose to commit, but real change unfolds when the deepest layers of your mind and heart buy in, when you become your own ally rather than your own saboteur. True commitment is less about willpower and more about alignment, gathering all the parts of yourself so that your yes is whole, not divided.

This is why old-school self-help advice, just declaring "I'll do it!" and pushing through, so often falls flat. If your unconscious is scared, resistant, or unconvinced, you will find ways to undermine yourself, no matter how strong your conscious desire. The real work is gentler: negotiating with all your inner voices, listening and soothing, making space for doubt and fear, and inviting them to join you rather than fighting them off.

Exercise: Getting Unconscious Buy-In

Find a quiet moment. Sit comfortably and place a hand on your heart or belly. Gently ask yourself: Is there any part of me that isn't ready to commit? Listen for whatever arises, words, images, sensations, or even silence.

If a resistant part emerges, get curious:

What is it afraid of?

What does it need in order to feel safe?

What would it like you to know, or do differently?

Thank every part of yourself for speaking, even the hesitant ones. If a part needs reassurance, gently negotiate: If I go slowly, can you come with me? Invite all of you into the commitment. Afterwards, write about the conversation in your journal.

Often, simply bringing resistance into the light softens its grip and begins to transform it into support. Each time you include another part of yourself, your commitment grows deeper and more sustainable, becoming not just a conscious promise, but a wholehearted agreement.

Exercises for Deepening Commitment

Ritualizing Your Yes

Ritual is how you make commitment visible, moving it from idea into the living, breathing world. You might write your commitment on a slip of paper and place it somewhere meaningful: tucked into your journal, on your altar, or taped to your mirror. Light a candle. Speak your yes out loud. Create a small gesture or symbol that embodies your devotion. Even the simplest rituals, repeated daily, can anchor your commitment and gently remind your unconscious that this is not just a thought but a living agreement with yourself.

Commitment Contracts

Some find it grounding to create a written commitment contract with themselves or with a trusted friend or mentor. This isn't about shame or pressure; it's about honoring your word with compassion and intention. Review your contract often, letting it evolve as you do. Here's a gentle template to guide you:

Sample Commitment Contract:

I, _____, commit to _____ for the next _____ days/weeks/months. My intention is _____. I will honor this commitment by _____. If I falter, I will return gently and begin again.

Signed: _____, Date: _____.

Commitment Circles

Bringing your commitment into community can amplify its power. Seek out a group, a partner, or a supportive circle where you can share your commitments, witness each other's progress, and hold space for encouragement and recommitment. Shared commitment is contagious: Your devotion strengthens the group, and the group's energy nourishes your own. There is magic in being seen, supported, and inspired as you walk the spiral of commitment together.

Micropractice

Choose one of the above exercises and gently try it on this week. Notice how the act of making your commitment visible and shared deepens your sense of yes.

How does it feel in your body, your heart, your mind?

Let each return, each ritual, each renewal be a celebration, not a chore.

THE SPIRAL OF COMMITMENT IN REAL LIFE

Commitment in its truest form is rarely linear. It spirals through our days and choices, sometimes bold, sometimes barely visible, always inviting us to return and begin again.

Jamie's Journey with BoundariesJamie, a health care provider, long struggled to set boundaries with colleagues and family. She worried that committing to her own well-being would be selfish, or create conflict. Together, we practiced *microcommitments*: saying no to just one request per week, setting her phone to Do Not Disturb for short intervals, journaling about the waves of guilt and relief that followed.

At first, Jamie's old story of being selfish was loud and persistent. But as she continued with these tiny acts, she noticed her body relaxing. More energy, better sleep, and, unexpectedly, gratitude from others, who admired her growing clarity and honesty, also came her way. Over time, these small commitments became natural. Jamie discovered that honoring herself allowed her to show up more authentically for everyone around her. The spiral of commitment, returning gently, forgiving setbacks, building capacity, became a quiet, steady presence in her life.

Malik's Dance With Consistency

Malik dreamed of writing a book, a vision that had haunted him for years. Paralyzed by the fear of imperfection, he started and stopped countless times. We shifted his focus away from achievement and toward the practice of returning, just fifteen minutes of writing a day, free from pressure or the need for perfection.

Malik learned to invite his whole self into the process: "I wonder what might happen if I just write, without worrying about the end result. Perhaps, even if I stop, I'll find myself returning with more ease." Each week, Malik celebrated his returns, not just his progress. Over time, writing became a trusted companion, and the first draft emerged not as a forced achievement but as the fruit of sustained, gentle commitment.

Invitation

Where do you see the spiral of commitment in your own life?

What microcommitments or gentle returns could you experiment with, allowing the process, not perfection, to guide you?

COMMITMENT IN COMMUNITY: THE WEB THAT HOLDS YOU

You do not commit in isolation. Every act of devotion is held within a web of relationships, seen and unseen, intimate and expansive. Whether it's a friend who checks in, a group that celebrates each milestone, or a mentor who reminds you why you began, community is the fertile ground where commitment is sustained and deepened.

When your energy fades or resistance grows, lean into your supports. Share your struggles and your victories. Allow others to witness your process, your stumbles as well as your strides. The spiral of commitment grows stronger through honest connection. When one member of a circle falters, another may offer encouragement, a gentle reminder, or the simple, steadfast presence that says, "You're not alone. You can begin again."

Community commitment takes many forms. Sometimes it is as simple as friends holding you accountable to a promise of self-care. Sometimes it is far larger, people linking arms, showing up for justice, and refusing to be silent in the face of harm. We see this in every generation when individuals and groups gather for dignity, safety, and belonging for all, often in the face of real resistance and risk. Such collective devotion, imperfect and vulnerable and courageous, reminds us that every voice matters and that we are woven together in a tapestry much greater than ourselves.

Prompt

Who are your commitment allies? What kind of support do you need to sustain your devotion? If you don't have this yet, what small step can you take to find or build it?

And, as you reflect, you might also ask: What cause, circle, or community would you be willing to stand for, even when the winds rise? Where could your commitment ripple outward, joining the greater web?

PERSEVERING THROUGH SETBACKS: THE ART OF RETURNING

No meaningful commitment is free from challenge. The spiral of transformation is lined with setbacks, stalls, and sometimes the aching temptation to quit. Even the most heartfelt yes will be tested by old patterns, new fears, or the simple fatigue that comes with walking a new path.

Here's what most transformation literature gets wrong: Setbacks are not evidence of a lack of commitment. They are the very terrain for which commitment exists. What distinguishes those who move through change from those who remain stuck isn't flawless progress, it's the willingness to return, again and again, to the center of their intention.

Every return is a quiet victory.

Even as you falter, you may notice that some part of you is still committed, perhaps more deeply than you realize. When you return after a lapse, whether a day, a week, or even years, the act of coming back reawakens the web of commitment and strengthens your capacity for resilience and renewal.

Exercise

Reflect on a time you fell off a commitment. What story did you tell yourself?

What if, instead of shame, you met yourself with curiosity:

What was needed? What was missing?

What would allow you to return?

Write about what it would feel like to meet every return with gentle celebration rather than criticism.

Leo's Return to Sobriety

Leo, in recovery from addiction, once saw relapse as catastrophic, a total failure of will. In our work, we reframed relapse as information: What was he needing? What warning signs did he ignore? How could he recommit more gently next time? By tracking patterns, seeking support, and forgiving himself, Leo's relapses became shorter, less shame filled, and his periods of commitment longer and more robust. Over time, Leo discovered that commitment was not about perfection but about the art of returning, each time, a little wiser, a little stronger.

Invitation

Is there a commitment in your life that could benefit from this shift in perspective?

How would your journey change if you saw every return not as evidence of failure but as a new spiral of possibility?

THE EVOLUTION OF COMMITMENT: GROWTH, CHANGE, AND LETTING GO

Commitment is not static. It is alive, growing, deepening, and sometimes needing to be released as you continue your spiral of becoming. There will be seasons when an old yes, maybe a job, a relationship, a creative pursuit, even a cherished spiritual practice, no longer fits. Outgrowing a commitment is not a failure; it is a sign of self-awareness and honest growth. Sometimes, the bravest act is not to double down but to pause, listen, and gently let go.

Letting go is its own form of commitment, a devotion to your authenticity, to the truth of who you are becoming. Just as a snake sheds its skin or a tree drops its leaves in autumn, you may be called to release what no longer serves, trusting that space will open for a new yes to emerge.

This process is not about abandoning responsibility but about honoring the wisdom that lives in your unconscious, listening inwardly for the subtle signals that a commitment needs refreshing, deepening, or perhaps tenderly ending. Sometimes you'll notice a quiet inner restlessness, a sense of being called elsewhere, or a growing gratitude for what has been, paired with readiness for what's next. Other times life will present changes beyond your control, asking you to renegotiate your promises with gentleness and courage.

To honor the evolution of your commitments is to honor your truth, your growth, and the living spiral of your own journey. Commitment, when fully alive, includes both the willingness to stay and the permission to release.

Prompt

Is there a commitment in your life that no longer aligns with who you are becoming?

How might you release it with gratitude, making space for a new yes?

Are there commitments asking for renewal, revision, or a tender ending?

Let yourself sit with these questions, perhaps in stillness, perhaps with your journal, listening for what your deepest wisdom is ready to reveal.

Integration: Practices for Deepening Commitment

Daily Commitment Ritual

Each morning, pause and rest a hand over your heart. Softly affirm:"Today, I recommit to _____. Even if I falter, I return. Each return is enough."

You might write it, speak it, or simply breathe it in. Let this gentle ritual become a source of steadiness, a way to remind yourself that commitment is a daily act, not a final destination.

Journal Practice: The Commitment Spiral

In your journal, draw a spiral beginning at the center. Along its path, mark each return, each wobble, every small act you've taken in service of your commitment. Track not only the moments of progress but also the process: when you recommitted, sought support, forgave yourself, or changed course. Over time, this visual map will become a testament to your perseverance, a gentle witness to your courage and devotion.

Witnessing and Celebration

Commitment grows stronger in the presence of others. Find a partner or a circle willing to witness your journey. Meet regularly to share your victories, your setbacks, your honest returns. Make celebration a practice not only when you reach completion but for every act of coming back. Each person's yes strengthens the web for all; each shared story weaves new threads of possibility.

Embodying Commitment

Bring your commitment into your body. Each time you recommit, press two fingers together or tap your chest, or use any simple kinesthetic anchor. Use it intentionally, linking the act of recommitting to a physical cue. Over days and weeks, this action becomes a gentle trance, a reminder to your body and mind of your devotion. The anchor grows stronger with each return, making commitment something you can feel as well as remember.

Invitation

Choose one of these practices to try for the next week. Notice how it shapes your experience of commitment, softening the inner critic, deepening your sense of belonging, making each return a cause for quiet celebration.

Let your commitment be spiral, embodied, and communal, a living agreement you renew, moment by moment, with kindness.

COMMITMENT AND FORGIVENESS: THE GENTLE RETURN

Self-forgiveness is perhaps the greatest act of commitment. Every spiral of growth includes disappointment and error, stumbles and detours. The practice is not in avoiding these moments but in how you meet yourself when they come. Each time you forgive yourself, you lay a new foundation, a way of being that is resilient, loving, and deeply real.

Forgiveness does not mean letting yourself off the hook, pretending nothing happened, or bypassing responsibility. Rather, it is the decision to choose growth over punishment, learning over regret, and love over fear. In the spiral of commitment, forgiveness is what makes it possible to return. It softens shame, quiets the inner critic, and opens the way to begin again, this time with more wisdom and gentleness.

When you forgive yourself, you are not erasing the past. You are honoring your full humanity: your longing, your mistakes, your efforts to change. You are declaring, "My commitment is not defined by perfection but by the courage to come back, again and again."

Forgiveness is not always easy. It may require grieving a lost ideal, feeling regret, or facing parts of yourself you wish you could ignore. You may need to forgive yourself for the same thing many times, each time revealing a new tenderness and a new capacity for growth. In this way, forgiveness becomes a living practice, a spiral, not a one-time event.

Forgiveness Ritual

When you are ready, write a letter of forgiveness to yourself. Begin: "Dear [Your Name], I forgive myself for ..."

Let your words be honest, raw, and unfiltered. Write until you feel something loosen, soften, or shift, even a little.

Afterwards, choose a ritual: Burn or bury the letter, letting the old story return to the earth, or keep it as a touchstone for your next return, a reminder that you have chosen love over fear.

Prompt

How might your journey change if you met each setback with forgiveness instead of criticism?

What is one thing you're ready to forgive yourself for today?

Let forgiveness be the gentle hand that welcomes you home. With each return, your commitment is not diminished. Instead, it is renewed, made deeper and more alive.

THE SPIRAL OF COMMITMENT: DEEPENING THE JOURNEY

It's easy to believe that commitment is a straight line: Start here, end there, and you're done. But the lived reality is much more like a spiral. Each return to your commitment brings you back, not to where you started but to a new place, deeper, wiser, and more compassionate for the detours, doubts, and discoveries that shaped you along the way.

The spiral is not a sign of failure or "not getting it right." In fact, it is living proof that you are alive and growing. Every time you return after a setback, a pause, or a period of wandering, you carry new perspective and understanding. What once looked impossible may seem ordinary now; what used to terrify you may become an effortless part of daily life. The path spirals outward, and with each loop, your view shifts.

Spiraling means that the old versions of you, the self who saw commitment only as willpower, rigidity, or all-or-nothing vows, can gently fall away. What remains is a relationship with yourself that is living, forgiving, and generous. This is the heart of the 5-Point Process: Each cycle through Vision, Commitment, Awareness, Living Into, and Integration brings new wisdom, humility, and strength.

Some days the spiral may feel tight, old patterns reemerge, and you wonder if you've truly changed. On other days, the spiral opens wide: You see your progress clearly, and you notice the quiet confidence that has grown in places where fear once lived. Neither moment is final; both are necessary.

Journal Prompt and Spiral Practice

Draw a spiral in your journal. Along its curve, note the commitments that have shaped you, the ones you kept, the ones you released, and the ones you revised as you grew. Mark the moments you wobbled, the places where you returned, and the points where you surprised yourself by showing up again when you were sure you could not.

As you reflect, look for patterns. What does this spiral reveal about your capacity for devotion, for forgiveness, and for beginning again?

What qualities do you bring to commitment now that you did not possess in earlier seasons of your life?

How might this living, spiraling map guide you as you move into what is next?

Let yourself be surprised by the resilience and wisdom that each return has woven into your life.

A Blessing for the Spiral
Pause here at this doorway.
Take a breath, let your shoulders soften, and open your heart
to everything you have returned to and everything that is
still becoming.
May you celebrate your journey so far:
the wobbles and the wins,
the lessons and the letting go,
the spirals that have carried you back, again and again, to the
center of your intention.
May you trust the spiral,
trust your courage to return,
your willingness to forgive,
your quiet devotion to beginning anew.

Let this be your blessing:
Every turn of the spiral is enough.
Every return is a victory.
You are not behind.
You are not unfinished.
You are not failing.
You are becoming, one gentle loop at a time.

COMMITMENT IN THE BODY: SOMATIC ANCHORING

Commitment is not just a mental process; it is deeply embodied. Your body is the ground where commitment becomes real. Notice what happens inside you when you say *yes*. Is there a settling, a quiet strength, or perhaps a flicker of tension? When you're tempted to give up, do you feel your chest tighten, your hands fidget, your breath grow shallow? Often, your nervous system holds the memory of old commitments gone wrong, or the ache of fearing disappointment, long before your mind catches up.

Somatic Practice

Pause. Place a hand over your heart or rest it on your solar plexus. Speak your commitment aloud, softly, just for you. Notice: Does your body want to move, contract, or relax? Let your attention rest gently on these sensations.

Now, invite your body to remember a time you honored a commitment, even in the face of challenge. How did that feel? Was there warmth, a sense of grounding, a breath of relief, a quiet pride? Allow your body to recall that feeling, even if it's subtle or fleeting. Imagine that yes spreading through your chest, your spine, your breath.

With each gentle repetition of this practice, you are teaching your nervous system to associate commitment with safety and self-trust rather than dread or pressure. Over time, this somatic anchor becomes a resource you can access, especially when the urge to flee, freeze, or give up arises. Repeating a small gesture: a breath, a touch, a movement, each time you recommit weaves body and mind together in devotion.

Let this be a trance you create for yourself, again and again:A felt sense of yes, alive in flesh and breath, always accessible, always yours.

Reflection

As you finish this practice, take one more slow breath. Notice the ripple, large or small, that a single moment of embodied commitment brings.

Ask yourself softly:

How does my yes feel in my body now? Where does it live?

How might returning to this anchor, especially on difficult days, change the way I meet my commitments?

Let your body remember that commitment is not only something you promise but something you practice and feel––one breath, one gesture, one return at a time.

ADVANCED PRACTICE: THE COMMITMENT TIMELINE

This practice invites you to step back and witness your journey with commitment as a living story, a path shaped by bright moments and shadows, detours and discoveries.

Timeline Practice

Take a sheet of paper and draw a horizontal line across the middle. Mark one end as the beginning of your journey with this particular commitment; the other end is today.

Begin to fill in the timeline with every key moment that stands out. Include moments of enthusiasm, clarity, and joy, as well as the hard ones; times you nearly quit, lost faith, or were tested by circumstances outside your control. Mark the places where support showed up or where a surprise or a helper made a difference. Don't rush; let the memories and feelings come in their own time.

Notice the patterns:

How long do you typically waver before you return?

Are there particular triggers that pull you off course, or signs that it's time to recommit?

Do your returns become easier, softer, or more frequent with time?

Pause, and look at your timeline as a whole. See the spiral in action—not a perfect line but a living journey with loops, pauses, and deepening insight.

Letter From Your Future Self

At the bottom of the page, write a letter from your future self, a version of you who has sustained, evolved, or even gently released this commitment.What does this future self know now?What wisdom can they offer about what truly matters, what lasts, and how to navigate the next spiral?

Let this letter be a source of encouragement, perspective, and gentle permission, guidance for your next return.

Reflection

What patterns or wisdom did you discover by looking at your timeline?

How did it feel to recognize the spiral, with all its setbacks and returns, as evidence of real devotion?

How might your future self walk with you as you continue to spiral deeper into your yes?

Let this practice be a touchstone, one you can return to any time your journey asks for perspective, compassion, or renewed courage.

ROADBLOCKS AND BREAKTHROUGHS: COMMITMENT CASE STUDIES

Every commitment journey encounters resistance, road-blocks, and surprising breakthroughs. These moments are not failures; they are invitations for deeper inquiry and growth. Here are two stories that show how commitment, when met with curiosity and compassion, becomes a path of self-acceptance and transformation.

Case 1: Anna's Sabbatical

Anna, a midcareer professor, dreamed for years of taking a creative sabbatical but could never quite commit. There was always another deadline, another email, a student who needed her attention. In our work, Anna began to see that her inability to commit was a form of self-protection: If she never fully said yes, she could never be disappointed or fail.

We explored her fears together, beginning with a simple question: "What is the worst that could happen if you allowed yourself a true sabbatical?" Anna journaled, visualized, and even dialogued with her inner critics. Gradually, she discovered her real longing: not just for time off but for a new, healthier relationship with her work and with herself. When Anna finally committed, not just on her calendar but in her bones, she noticed something astonishing: Her department head approved her request with enthusiasm, and colleagues expressed both envy and admiration. Anna's breakthrough was not about scheduling or logistics but about giving herself permission to matter, to honor her own needs and dreams.

Case 2: Jason's Parenting Promise

Jason, a single father, struggled with being present for his children after long shifts. His old commitment style was perfectionistic––if he missed an evening story, he'd feel like a failure and often spiral into disengagement. Through our sessions, Jason learned to view commitment as an evolving practice, not an absolute standard.

He began to create small, sacred rituals: a five-minute check-in, a weekly "adventure walk." He kept a log of his returns, times he repaired a missed connection by apologizing, starting anew, or simply asking, "How can I be here with you now?" Over time, his children learned to trust the pattern: Dad doesn't always get it right, but he always comes back. The bond deepened, not despite imperfection but because of it. Jason's real commitment was not to unbroken performance but to a relationship built on repair, humility, and love.

Reflection

What roadblocks or fears have stood between you and a whole-hearted commitment?

Is there a longing beneath your resistance, a need for permission, acceptance, or a gentler standard?

How might you, like Anna or Jason, let your next breakthrough be not about doing it perfectly but about returning, repairing, and choosing yourself or your loved ones anew?

WHEN COMMITMENT FEELS IMPOSSIBLE: SHADOW WORK

Every meaningful commitment will eventually encounter resistance. The deeper your *yes*, the more likely you are to meet the inner *no*––the fears, doubts, and old stories that whisper at the edges of your courage. Jung called this the shadow: the parts of ourselves we'd rather avoid or disown but that hold wisdom and energy if we're willing to listen.

Shadow work is the practice of inviting these partsa: your fears, doubts, objections, and even your harshest inner critic, into the circle. Not to do battle but to make peace. Sometimes, resistance is simply an old story echoing from childhood, a parent's voice or a cultural warning: "Why bother?" "Who do you think you are?" Other times, it's the body's memory of disappointment or a longing for safety disguised as sabotage.

The work here is to bring these voices to the table, gently and with curiosity. Ask:

"What are you protecting?"

"What do you want for me?"

"How might you help if we work together?"

This is the deeper spiral of commitment: turning enemies into allies, integrating your inner critics until they become part of your team, offering caution and perspective instead of opposition.

Prompt

List every fear, doubt, and objection you have about your current commitment.

Write a brief conversation with each one. Ask, "If I honor you, what gift might you offer?"

Imagine inviting your resistance to walk beside you rather than stand in your way.

Let your commitment become a place of integration, not a battlefield but a living agreement between all the parts of yourself. This is where true, sustainable commitment is born, in the willingness to bring the whole of you on the journey.

SPIRITUALITY AND COMMITMENT: THE MYSTERY BEYOND THE SELF

For many, commitment is more than a personal act, it is a spiritual one. There is a kind of sacredness in saying yes, a sense that your devotion does not end with you but ripples outward into the wider web of the world. Whether you name this web God, Spirit, the universe, destiny, or simply the field of possibility, each commitment is a prayer, an offering, a seed planted in the soil of the collective.

W.H. Murray's wisdom, "then Providence moves too," reminds us that there are forces beyond our conscious will that respond when we act from the core of our being. You may notice this in small synchronicities or in great, mysterious waves: The right person appears, a door opens, resources find their way to you, or sudden clarity descends. These moments are not mere coincidences but the natural response of life to a clear, heartfelt yes.

Many people share that when they finally commit fully, in body, mind, and spirit, life begins to meet them halfway. Old obstacles dissolve, or the courage to face them deepens. There is a feeling of being partnered, accompanied, no longer alone in the journey. Even if you do not identify with a particular spiritual tradition, you may sense that every commitment is an act of trust: Trust that your yes matters and that it will be met by something larger than yourself.

Commitment, in this light, becomes a living conversation, a dance between your intention and the world's mysterious reply. Each time you choose devotion over hesitation, you join in the great spiral of becoming, moving not only yourself but the fabric of reality, one quiet yes at a time.

COMMITMENT TO COMMUNITY AND JUSTICE

Some commitments, such as health, creativity, relationships, are deeply personal. Others reach outward, becoming social, ethical, or even revolutionary. In a world that so often rewards individual gain, to commit to community, justice, or the healing of the greater whole is an act of vision and courage. These commitments can feel daunting, even lonely, especially when results are slow or invisible. Yet, every small act is a thread woven into the fabric of collective transformation.

Your commitment, whether public or quiet, bold or humble, can become a seed for change in the lives of others, even if you never see the final harvest. When you advocate for a cause, mentor someone younger, show up for those on the margins, or simply offer your presence, you are helping to build a web of trust, hope, and resilience. The effect is rarely linear or immediate, but over time your devotion will help hold the world together.

Case Example

Maria, a bilingual therapist, committed to offering free workshops in her local immigrant community. Turnout was small at first, and she often questioned whether her efforts were making a difference. Still, she kept showing up, offering her skills and her heart. Gradually, word spread. People began to share her resources, and other professionals joined. What began as one person's devotion grew into a small movement, proof that even the quietest commitments can animate a much larger field.

Reflection

Where might your yes to justice, inclusion, or community be quietly needed?

What cause or group calls for your presence, even if the outcome is uncertain?

Remember: Every act of commitment, no matter how small, is a thread in the web of belonging.

LOOKING AHEAD: COMMITMENT AS A LIFELONG PRACTICE

As you reach the end of this chapter, remember: Commitment is never truly finished. It is a living practice, a spiral, a promise you renew with each new breath and season. The work of committing and recommitting, again and again, builds your capacity to stay awake to life, to love more deeply, and to live ever more fully in alignment with who you are becoming.

You are not asked to be perfect, only to return. Each return is an act of devotion, evidence that your yes still matters, and that your life is worthy of your own trust.

In the next chapter, "Awareness," you'll explore how to notice and honor the changes, the signs, and the subtle movements that arise as you continue the spiral. Commitment opens the door; awareness will help you see the terrain and navigate with increasing clarity, curiosity, and trust.

Final Exercise:

Set aside time this week to gently revisit every commitment you hold, large and small. Which are still alive? Which are asking for letting go, revision, or deepening? Make a list. For each, softly ask yourself, "What is my next, most loving step?"

When you are ready, share at least one of your commitments with someone you trust. Let them witness your yes, and offer to witness theirs in return. Let this act of shared witnessing be a blessing, a reminder that your journey is always supported and that you never walk alone.

A Blessing for the Spiral of Commitment

May you celebrate your willingness to begin and begin again.
May each return to your yes bring you closer to your own
heart.
May your devotion ripple outward, nourishing the world
around you.
And may you trust that every spiral, no matter how winding,
brings you closer to the life that calls you forward.

7. AWARENESS: STEP 3 OF THE 5-POINT PROCESS

The curious paradox is that when I accept myself just as I am, then I can change.

— CARL ROGERS

The boundary to what we can accept is the boundary to our freedom.

— TARA BRACH

THE SPIRAL PATH OF AWARENESS

THERE IS a moment in every journey, whether healing, learning, or simply living, when you realize you have been moving from a script you did not consciously write. Sometimes it is a subtle twinge in your chest at a dinner party. Sometimes it is hearing words slip from your mouth that sound like someone else entirely. These moments, gentle or jarring, are where awareness quietly begins to change everything.

For me, awareness is the art of catching myself midscript, pausing, and softly asking, *What is really happening here?* Without it, I move through life on autopilot, shaped by habit, old stories, or the tide of circumstance. With awareness, I become a quiet witness, a gentler presence within myself, available for choice, healing, and the possibility of something new.

You have seen this throughout the book: Vision is the invitation. Commitment is the declaration. Awareness is where the real work and the real magic begin. This is where you discover, again and again, that you can be both the author and the observer of your story. That change is born not from striving but from seeing, naming, and allowing what is.

As you move through this chapter, let the teachings about acceptance and freedom spiral through your awareness, inviting you to ask: *Where might deeper seeing and deeper acceptance widen the boundaries of my own freedom, both within myself and in the world I touch?*

WHAT AWARENESS REALLY IS (AND ISN'T)

Many people confuse awareness with analysis or self-critique, imagining it requires constant vigilance and scanning for every flaw. But that is not the awareness I invite. True awareness is a soft, steady returning. It is the willingness to let your experience be what it is, met with curiosity and as much kindness as you can offer. It is noticing without rushing to fix. Sometimes it is even noticing the urge to fix and letting that be part of the moment.

Awareness is a living spiral, not a straight line. There will be days when you see clearly and respond with grace. There will also be days when you forget, lose yourself, or slip into old reactions. This is not failure. It is the practice. Forgetting and remembering, noticing and returning, this is the rhythm that strengthens awareness over time.

Carl Rogers teaches that when we accept ourselves as we are, even in our forgetfulness and striving, genuine change becomes possible. Tara Brach reminds us that the edge of what we can accept is the edge of our freedom. Awareness is not about staying on guard. It is about allowing, widening, and including more of your actual, present-moment experience.

Some days awareness feels like a quiet light, gently revealing what was hidden. Other days it is a small act of courage, softening your heart toward yourself when you notice you are caught in an old pattern. Either way, every return is a sign of devotion. Each spiral is a doorway into greater presence and liberation.

MY STORIES: FROM PARTIES TO PARENTS

The Party and the "Figure It Out" Moment

I recently went to a friend's party. The evening was lively, with music and animated conversation, Spanish and English blending together. As often happens when I am the only nonfluent Spanish speaker, I hovered at the edges, grateful when someone leaned in to quietly translate.

As the night unfolded, something surprised me. During a story told in Spanish, my friend began translating for me. Suddenly another guest, who had been drinking heavily, cut in: "Don't translate for him. He should have to figure it out for himself, just like I did at my job. That's how you learn."

No one else seemed to notice, but I felt heat rise in my face and a tightening in my chest. My first instinct was to retreat. I left soon after, feeling both invisible and strangely exposed. Awareness arrived later, when irritation bubbled under the surface and I replayed the moment.

What surfaced was not just the man's comment. It was the memory of every time I had felt on the outside: gay, over-weight, the kid scanning the room to decide what was safe. In an instant I was ten years old again, shrinking at the sound of laughter I did not understand, rehearsing how to blend in or avoid being noticed for the wrong reason.

When awareness settled, it brought pain and clarity. The sting remained: sadness, disappointment, and a quiet appre-hension about seeing this man again. Beneath it all lived a sense of betrayal—not only by him, but by those who, in my mind, did nothing to defend me, even though I know that was not their job.

My body, mind, and history responded together in an old, automatic defense that once kept me safe. Now, with aware-ness, I can see these layers for what they are. I am not ten anymore. I can honor those wounds while noticing the stories I carry and gently updating them. This is the spiral at work: staying present for old feelings, making new choices, and practicing the possibility of responding differ-ently next time, even if only by staying with myself more kindly.

Acceptance becomes the doorway to change, and the edge of what we can accept often becomes the edge of our freedom. Awareness does not erase discomfort. It offers a way to meet it with tenderness and a wider embrace.

The "Why Aren't You Married?" Conversation

Earlier that same evening, another stranger cornered me with questions that felt both innocent and invasive: "Why aren't you married? Were you divorced? What happened?" He pressed on, undeterred by my polite deflection, as if singlehood were a problem to solve.

Again, I felt myself shrink, answering just enough to pass, feeling the familiar urge to justify my existence. Later, I remembered that I am allowed to set a boundary. I could have said, "I'm not comfortable sharing that." In the moment, I did not have the words. But in the spiral of awareness, I could notice my discomfort, forgive myself, and practice a kinder, clearer response for next time.

This is awareness at work: recognizing your edges, accepting what you feel, and moving the boundary of your freedom outward.

My Parents and the Real Doctor Story

Awareness is also about recognizing what we inherit. When I told my parents, with great excitement, that I wanted to become a psychologist, their response was immediate: "So you're not going to be a real doctor? We never knew anyone who went to a psychologist and got any help."

I felt crushed. Their voices became a quiet echo inside me, shaping how I measured my worth for years. Sometimes I overworked to prove them wrong. Sometimes I shrank, doubting myself.

With years of awareness practice, journaling, and reflection, I learned to see their reaction in a new light. It was never really a judgment on my path; it was a mirror of their fears, their generational beliefs, and their misunderstandings about mental health. Their voices remain, but now they sit within a much wider inner chorus rather than directing it.

Invitation

Perhaps now and then you will notice when an old script begins to take the lead. In those moments, you might pause and ask, What is true for me right now? Let awareness be like a gentle hand on your shoulder. There is no need to rush or force anything. Simply noticing and softly returning begins to loosen old patterns and make room for something new.

As your spiral of awareness unfolds, it becomes less about getting anything right and more about being present, softening, and allowing change to come in its own time. Every gentle return is already transformation.

ON CULTURE, BELONGING, AND THE SPIRAL OF AWARENESS

As I reflect on these stories, I am struck by how deeply our sense of belonging, or feeling like an outsider, is shaped by the cultures we are born into and the cultures we step into later in life. Some of what was activated for me at that party traces back to early wounds: family messages about success, the ache of unmet expectations, the tension of being different in my own home. Other feelings arise from living as a guest in a culture that is not my own, where language, humor, customs, and subtle gestures often carry meanings I cannot fully access.

Warmth and community are abundant in México, yet the unspoken social codes and boundaries sometimes feel mysterious. What feels normal to me may land differently here, and what feels like rejection may simply belong to a different cultural script. I often forget that I am navigating not only my own history but also a set of norms I am still learning, often without a map.

This awareness is humbling. My personal spiral of noticing, hurting, and healing is unfolding inside a larger dance of cultures, languages, and expectations. Realizing this does not make my feelings less real. Instead, it helps me hold them with greater humility and curiosity. Each discomfort, whether rooted in my past or in the present moment of cultural difference, becomes an invitation to pause, inquire, and expand my capacity for compassion.

Awareness gives me permission to honor these layers. Belonging becomes a practice, both within myself and in the places I hope to call home.

Every unfamiliar moment becomes a call to soften, to include more of my own experience and more of those around me. In this way, the spiral of awareness becomes both personal and communal, guiding me toward a wider and more generous freedom.

THE PRACTICE OF AWARENESS: ART, SCIENCE, AND SPIRIT

Awareness is more than a tool. It is a way of being, a quiet courage that reshapes us from the inside out. From a neuroscience perspective, each moment of noticing builds new pathways in the brain, softening the grip of habit and reactivity. Mindful, embodied attention strengthens the prefrontal cortex and helps regulate the limbic system, creating more room for choice and a fuller experience of the present moment. In a very real way, awareness becomes a practice of freedom at the level of biology. Each gentle return to noticing literally expands the paths our lives can take.

Yet awareness is older and deeper than anything brain science can map. It is the root of every wisdom tradition, a living current that flows through cultures across the world, each giving it its own language, rituals, and metaphors.

In Buddhism, mindfulness is both refuge and path, bringing insight, compassion, and a sense of interbeing. In Christianity, the invitation to watch and pray asks us to stay awake to our thoughts, choices, and the subtle movement of grace. Jewish traditions offer hitbodedut, a practice of honest conversation with the Divine, and daily reflection through prayer and study. In Islamic Sufism, muraqaba, or watchful and loving attention, opens the way to the Divine both within and beyond.

Among the First Nations of Turtle Island and many Indigenous communities worldwide, awareness is sacred seeing, an embodied knowing that each of us is a thread in the living web. It calls us to listen to the land, the ancestors, and to what is unsaid as much as what is spoken. The Zulu teaching of ubuntu, "I am because we are," reminds us that awareness is fundamentally relational. To be awake is to be alive to the needs, joys, and suffering of those around us.

Even within a single country, traditions of awareness take many forms. In México, daily life is rich with practices of sacred noticing: the morning altar, greeting neighbors, the ritual of preparing food, and the collective honoring of ancestors during Día de muertos. Each invites us to pay attention, to remember, and to participate in something larger than ourselves. In the United States, Quaker silent meetings, African American spirituals, Appalachian storytelling, and protest and collective action all become spaces where noticing the self, the community, and the moment opens the door to change.

Modern psychology has its own lineages. Jungian shadow work invites us to turn gently toward what we would rather not see. Somatic therapies, mindfulness-based approaches, and trauma-informed practices use awareness as the ground of healing, giving us a way to witness pain without being swallowed by it.

Across every tradition, awareness becomes the key to freedom. Not because it erases pain or offers total control, but because it makes everything available to be met, felt, understood, and transformed. In a world where freedom can feel fragile, where cultural forces or political decisions threaten our sense of agency, awareness becomes a form of resistance and renewal. No law or authority can take away your capacity to notice, reflect, or choose your next response. In this sense, awareness is the last freedom, the inner space where dignity, compassion, and meaning remain possible even when outer circumstances are uncertain.

To practice awareness is to join a lineage as old as humanity. Even in dark moments, it is possible to awaken, to see, to remember, and to live as if freedom and belonging are not only possible but your birthright.

EVERYDAY AWARENESS: PAINTING THE MOMENTS

In the Kitchen

There is awareness in the simple act of chopping vegetables, in the sound of the knife, the scent of garlic, the way your breath changes with each slice. Notice where you rush and where you slow down, and what memories or emotions food stirs in you. Cooking can become a quiet meditation, a time for gentle self-talk and honest reflection. What would it be like to let each sensation, thought, and feeling simply belong, without needing to change it?

In Nature

Take a walk with the intention to notice rather than accomplish. Let your eyes, ears, and skin guide you. Pay attention to warmth or chill, to colors you might otherwise overlook, to the way the world shifts when you stop narrating it and simply let it be. Nature draws us into presence and invites us to slow down, creating space for awareness to unfold naturally.

With Others

Experiment with awareness the next time you are in conversation. Notice your tone, your breath, your posture. Are you leaning in or pulling away? Listening deeply or rehearsing your reply? Do you long to be seen, or are you guarding something tender? Bring soft attention to the ways you protect yourself and to the moments when you allow yourself to be fully present with another person.

Practices for Deepening Awareness

Introducing the Awareness Spiral

Throughout this chapter, the spiral has been a metaphor for how we return to ourselves again and again. Here, it becomes a practice. The Awareness Spiral is a simple, repeatable process you can use anytime you want to meet your experience with clarity and compassion. Think of it as a gentle map for turning toward yourself.

The Awareness Spiral (Guided Practice)

Pause: Take three slow breaths.

Notice: Scan your body, emotions, thoughts, and surroundings.

Name: Say or write, "I notice _____."

Allow: Sit with what is present without trying to change it. "It is okay that _____ is here."

Dialogue: If a feeling is strong, ask it, "What are you protecting? What do you want me to know?"

Choose: Ask, "What is needed now?" Let the answer arise naturally, even if it is small.

Return: Thank yourself for noticing. Let this be enough for now.

Advanced Prompt

Try practicing the Awareness Spiral with a friend or in a journaling group. Share what arises and listen for what feels universal and what is uniquely your own.

Awareness in Groups: The Awareness Circle

Gather with a few trusted people. Take turns sharing an experience from your day, focusing only on noticing, naming, and allowing. When others listen, their only response is to share what they noticed in themselves. For example, "When you spoke, I felt a tightness in my chest." This kind of circle builds a field of collective presence, deepening both individual awareness and group safety.

Awareness and the Body

Your body is often your first teacher. Each ache, flutter, or breath is a doorway into awareness. Try body mapping once a week:

Sit quietly and scan upward from your feet, noticing sensations, tension, warmth, or ease.

When you encounter a sensation, pause and ask, "What do you want me to notice?"

Thank your body, even if the message is not yet clear.

With time, this practice reveals patterns in your stress, emotions, and joy.

Reflection

Notice which practice gently draws your attention. There is no need to choose quickly; simply let your awareness settle where it wishes.

As you rest into these small moments, observe what opens for you. Even a brief pause can create a bit more space, a touch more kindness, a new sense of freedom inside. Let yourself be quietly surprised by what emerges when you meet your experience with curiosity and possibility.

PHILOSOPHICAL DEPTH: AWARENESS AS PATH

From both spiritual and developmental perspectives, awareness is the fertile ground from which all genuine growth emerges. Every tradition that explores the inner life has its own way of naming this possibility: waking up to what is, both within and around us.

In Sufism, awakening is described as the ability to see clearly, without distortion or defense. This clarity is not a single achievement but a spiral of returning, again and again, to presence, humility, and the simple truth available in each moment.

Somatic psychology teaches that sensation is often the first medicine. Awareness of the body becomes an anchor that helps us regulate, recognize trauma responses, and gently find our way back to safety and belonging. Sometimes, pausing to feel your breath or the ground beneath your feet is enough to restore a sense of resilience and to reopen the possibility of feeling at home.

Mindfulness traditions, Buddhist and otherwise, describe awareness as both the beginning and the end of the journey. It is noticing what is, just as it is, without rushing to judge or change it. The Zen saying, "Before enlightenment, chop wood, carry water. After enlightenment, chop wood, carry water," reminds us that presence transforms even the most ordinary act into an opportunity for meaning.

Yet you do not need to belong to any particular tradition to practice awareness. All that is required is curiosity, a willingness to pause, and an openness to what is already here. Awareness is spacious and democratic, available in any moment and to anyone, regardless of background, belief, or circumstance. Whether you are sitting on a meditation cushion, walking through the park, or washing dishes, awareness is waiting for you. It is a quiet invitation to meet your life as it unfolds and to discover, again and again, that awakening is possible right here, right now.

Reflection

Notice what it feels like to bring a bit more curiosity or softness into your day. What happens if, instead of striving or judging, you rest in presence and let it unfold naturally? Let this be an invitation to welcome what is already here and to trust that presence will find you, just as you are.

REFLECTIONS ON FORGETTING AND REMEMBERING

Every day, you will forget. This is not a flaw or a failure; it is simply part of being human. No matter how much intention you set or how deeply committed you are, you will lose your way again. You will slip into old habits, find yourself reacting instead of responding, drift into autopilot, or momentarily believe a story that no longer fits who you are becoming.

Sometimes you will notice the forgetting right away, a sudden awareness that you have gone numb, taken on someone else's expectations, or begun replaying an old wound. Other times hours or even days may pass before you realize how far you have wandered from the person you long to be. In those moments you might feel frustrated or disappointed, convinced you have fallen back into the same place yet again. But if you look closely, you will see that this, too, is part of the path.

And then, quietly or all at once, you remember. Sometimes the remembering is soft, like the landing of a bird: a breath, a word, a moment of presence. Sometimes it arrives with force, as if life is tapping you on the shoulder and asking, "Is this still where you want to be?" However it comes, each moment of remembering is a threshold, a return to awareness, a coming home to yourself.

The rhythm of forgetting and remembering is the spiral that shapes a life aligned. It is never linear. You do not graduate from forgetting. Instead, you learn to recognize it sooner, to return with less judgment and more kindness. The episodes of forgetting grow shorter and the moments of remembering grow gentler. You become more skilled at noticing and beginning again. What once felt like failure reveals itself as an essential part of the practice.

With every loop of the spiral, you bring new perspective. The sting of old patterns softens, and the celebration of each return deepens. You discover that the goal was never to arrive at some fixed point but to participate fully in the dance, honoring both the wandering and the return. The more often you practice returning, the more natural it becomes. You do not need to get it perfect. You simply need to keep showing up, again and again.

Let this be your reminder: Forgetting is not a problem to solve but an invitation to come home as many times as you need. Remembering is a quiet victory each time you notice, even for a moment, what is true for you now. The magic is not in never losing your way but in cultivating the capacity to meet yourself kindly wherever you find yourself and to begin again.

This is the spiral: always returning, never quite to the same place, each time a little wiser, a little softer, and a little more aligned with the life that is yours to live.

The Many Faces of Awareness in Healing and Growth

The Student Who Couldn't Meditate

A few years ago, Lila (not her real name), a doctoral student of mine, shared her frustration with mindfulness assignments. "When I try to meditate, my mind races, and I just feel like a failure," she admitted during class, her voice holding both defeat and a quiet longing for relief.

We explored what was happening in her Awareness Spiral. It turned out she was not failing at all. She was simply noticing more. Her mind had always raced, but now she was finally witnessing it instead of being swept away. The practice of noticing was both unsettling and hopeful.

We reframed her goal: Instead of trying to stop her thoughts, what if she became a friendly witness to them? Could she allow the swirl without collapsing into it? By the end of the semester, Lila reported that her mind still raced, but she could now pause and say, "There goes my mind again," with a half-smile instead of a groan. Awareness did not change her mind overnight, but it loosened the grip of old habits and gave her the dignity of not needing to be perfect in order to grow.

Awareness and the Edge of Trauma

In therapy, awareness becomes a bridge to healing, but it is also a place to tread with great care. I recall working with Joseph, a survivor of early childhood neglect. He had learned to cope by disconnecting from his body, living mostly in thoughts and future plans. Our early work was not about uncovering memories but about building his capacity for gentle noticing.

When Joseph practiced simple awareness, whether noticing the weight of his body in the chair or the coolness of air on his skin, he sometimes felt a rush of panic or a slide into numbness. We slowed everything down. We honored his nervous system. We celebrated each moment that felt safe. I would remind him, "It is okay to go only as far as feels safe, and then rest."

Joseph's healing spiral was slow and gentle. Sometimes it was frustrating, but it was always guided by one question: "Can I notice one thing, right now, that lets me know I am safe?" Over time, those moments grew. The capacity for presence without overwhelm became the clearest evidence of his healing.

Awareness as Group Practice

Awareness, while deeply personal, is also profoundly collective. In my professional circles, we sometimes begin meetings with a minute of silence, simply noticing our breath, our bodies, and the shared energy of the room. It shifts everything. Decisions become clearer. Misunderstandings soften. Creativity emerges more easily from the space that awareness opens.

Families can practice this too. Even young children respond to simple invitations: "Let's take one deep breath before dinner," or "Can we each name one feeling we had today?" These small rituals help everyone build the muscle of presence and show that there is room to notice, to feel, and to share what is real.

Awareness and Relationships: Mirrors and Magnets

So much of our growth happens in relationship, whether romantic, familial, collegial, or casual. Awareness is the key that turns reactivity into response. When we bring curiosity to our triggers, we loosen our grip on the story and begin to see ourselves in context.

Maria and the Difficult Conversation

Maria, a coaching client, dreaded conflict. When her partner raised an issue, she would shut down or lash out, unsure how to stay present with her emotions. Together we practiced the Awareness Spiral in real time so she could use it during these moments. Here is what it looked like for her:

Pause: Feel your feet on the ground.

Notice: Bring attention to your breath and the rhythm of your heartbeat.

Name: After a moment, gently identify what is present. "I notice a tightness in my chest… I think I'm feeling angry and scared."

Allow: Let the sensations be there, without pushing them away or acting on them.

Express: When ready, speak from awareness. "I'm noticing I feel overwhelmed, and I want to stay with this if we can."

The first few attempts were messy. There were tears, long silences, and sometimes an early exit from the conversation. But with practice, Maria found she could remain present a bit longer each time. Awareness began turning what once felt like a battleground into a space for honesty, tenderness, and real connection.

Reflection

Notice where the spiral of awareness has appeared in your own healing or relationships, those moments of forgetting, noticing, returning, and responding. Imagine what it might feel like to trust that even the smallest act of noticing is a sign of growth. Let your journey be gentle, imperfect, and powerful in its own way. Each return is enough.

Awareness and Trauma: Permission to Go Slow

For those with a trauma history, awareness is both vital and potentially overwhelming. Even simple noticing can spark strong body reactions such as shame, fear, or the urge to escape your experience. This is not a sign of failure. It is a natural response. In these moments, awareness is not about pushing through discomfort. It is about titrating your attention and honoring your own pace.

Practice: Gentle Titration

When a strong feeling or memory arises, allow yourself to turn away or take a break if you need to.

Anchor yourself in the present. Notice your feet on the ground, look around the room, and name a few objects or colors you see.

Return to awareness only when you are ready, even if it is for a few seconds at a time.

Seek support whenever possible from trusted friends, therapists, or guides. Healing does not happen in isolation.

Every safe return to awareness, however brief, is a triumph. You are allowed to move at your own pace. Even the smallest moments of presence become seeds of resilience and healing.

Reflection

How might it feel to give yourself permission to go slower, to rest, or to seek support as you move through your own spiral of healing?

What would happen if you trusted that even the smallest return is enough for today?

Let that be your quiet encouragement, exactly as you are.

THE SCIENCE OF AWARENESS: HOW NOTICING CHANGES THE BRAIN

Decades of research now confirm what mindfulness and healing traditions have long taught: Awareness rewires the brain. Each small act of noticing, every moment of gentle attention, creates real and lasting change in your mind and body.

Neural pathways:

Each time you notice what is happening, whether it is a breath, a thought, or an emotion, you strengthen new neural connections. This supports the prefrontal cortex, which helps regulate emotion and allows you to choose how to respond. Over time, these new patterns soften the grip of old habits and emotional reactions.

Resilience:

People who practice awareness recover more quickly from stress, manage pain with greater ease, and report higher levels of well-being. Awareness helps you meet difficulty with more internal resources and less overwhelm, expanding your capacity for resilience.

Choice:

Noticing interrupts the autopilot of habit. Instead of reacting unconsciously, you create a small space between what happens and how you respond. In that space, new choices become possible. You begin to respond rather than react, and this opens possibilities for your life and relationships.

You are not simply the product of your past. With awareness, you become the sculptor of your present and your future. Each gentle return to noticing is both a biological and a spiritual act of freedom, shaping who you are becoming one moment at a time.

Reflection

What small act of awareness might you invite into your day today? Even a few gentle breaths of noticing can open new space for choice, healing, or compassion. Let that possibility unfold quietly, just for today.

AWARENESS IN ORDINARY LIFE: SCENES AND SCRIPTS

Awareness does not belong only to meditation cushions or therapy sessions. It lives in the scenes and scripts of daily life, waiting for your gentle attention.

In the Kitchen

As you chop onions, pause and notice the scent, the sting in your eyes, the rhythm of your knife. Are you rushing or savoring the process? Who taught you to cook this way? What stories about food or care rise for you? Each moment in the kitchen can become a doorway to awareness, inviting you to feel not only what you are doing but how you are being.

On the Commute

Sitting in traffic, you might feel impatience or boredom. Awareness invites you to scan your body. Are your hands tense on the wheel? Are your shoulders lifted, your jaw tight? Notice what changes when you soften your grip or let your shoulders drop. The commute becomes an opportunity for presence, a window into your habits and needs.

In Relationships

A friend texts you in a tone that feels off. You notice the urge to reply quickly or defensively. Pause and sense what is underneath. Is it irritation, hurt, confusion? Name it to yourself. Allow it to be there without rushing to fix or hide it. Awareness gives you space to choose your response instead of falling into an old reflex. Sometimes the most skillful reply is simply, "I need a moment," and that is enough.

Invitation

Where in your daily routines might you bring a soft moment of noticing? You could wonder what shifts when ordinary moments become invitations to awareness rather than tasks to complete. Each small act of noticing deepens your presence. Let new ways of living find you, one gentle breath at a time.

GROUP AWARENESS: THE POWER OF CIRCLES

Awareness deepens when it is shared. Forming an awareness circle with friends, family, or colleagues can become a powerful ground for healing, growth, and genuine community. These circles create a space where the simple act of noticing, without judgment or advice, becomes a kind of collective medicine.

Try meeting regularly, in person or online, with only one agenda: to practice noticing, naming, and allowing together.

Begin with a breath or a moment of silence, allowing everyone to arrive and settle.

Each person shares something they have noticed about themselves––a feeling, a habit, a reaction, or a moment of forgetting and remembering.

The others simply listen, offering presence and witness rather than advice or fixing.

Close by offering gratitude for each person's honesty and willingness to show up as they are.

Over time, these circles can model a new kind of culture, one where awareness, not perfection, is the norm. The circle itself becomes a spiral of learning, where each participant's story invites the group to deepen their own noticing. As trust builds, the power of collective awareness ripples outward, reminding us that we are not alone on our journey.

Invitation

If you feel drawn, consider gathering a few trusted people and trying this simple circle. Notice how sharing and witnessing, with no pressure to change or fix, can open space for acceptance and belonging.

Let group awareness weave itself into your own spiral, becoming a quiet part of your larger community.

AWARENESS AND THE SEASONS OF LIFE

Your capacity for awareness, whether of the year, your life, or your own healing spiral, will naturally shift with the seasons. Some periods call for deep introspection that draws you inward to notice and reflect. Other seasons ask for rest, a pause in practice, or a turning outward toward distraction or action.

It is completely natural for your awareness practice to ebb and flow. Trust that every return matters, even when it is brief or infrequent. Just as spring follows winter, your spiral will always bring you back to presence, often in the moments you least expect. This gentle rhythm of deepening and resting, returning and growing, is part of what makes awareness so alive and resilient.

Journal Reflection

What season of awareness are you in right now? Are you deepening, resting, returning, or growing?

How might you honor this season just as it is, trusting that awareness will call you back in its own time?

Let yourself be exactly where you are. Awareness, like the seasons, unfolds in its own way.

Advanced Practices: Awareness Journeys

If you feel ready to deepen your spiral of awareness, these practices can support you in exploring new domains of your daily life and guide you beyond the mind into the wisdom of the body.

The Seven-Day Awareness Challenge

Body — Track physical sensations as you move through the day. Notice tension, ease, hunger, warmth, coolness, and subtle shifts.

Emotions — Pause each hour, or as often as you remember, to name your dominant emotion. Notice how it changes or repeats.

Thoughts — Observe your habitual thought patterns. When do you notice worries, judgments, or daydreams? Can you gently trace what seems to trigger them?

Relationships — Bring soft awareness to one key interaction. Notice your body, your tone, and what you are longing for or holding back.

Work or Creativity — Pay attention to your energy, focus, and patterns. Where do you feel most alive, and where do you get stuck or distracted?

Nature — Spend time outdoors, even briefly. Practice "bare attention": see, listen, and feel without labeling or fixing.

Silence — Dedicate a little time to stillness or meditation, even a few minutes. Notice what arises in the quiet, without judgment.

At the end of each day, journal about what you learned, what surprised you, and how awareness shaped your choices or experience.

Awareness Through Art and Movement

Some insights arrive through the body and hands, not only through the mind. Let these practices open new doors for noticing, expression, and self-kindness.

Movement

Try a slow walk, gentle yoga, or free-form dance with the intention to feel each sensation. Notice how emotion moves through your body. Where do you feel resistance or ease? What begins to shift as you move?

Art

Doodle, paint, or sculpt. Allow your hands to express what your words cannot. When you finish, look gently at what you created. What feelings, memories, or stories arise? How can you meet them with curiosity and kindness?

Let these practices deepen your relationship with awareness. There is no correct way to do them. The invitation is simply to notice, include, and accept more of your experience as it unfolds.

Reflection

How might play, movement, or art open new awareness for you?

What might you discover if you step outside routine and let something unexpected show you the way?

Let yourself be quietly curious.

AWARENESS AS SPIRITUAL PRACTICE

Across cultures and ages, awareness has been understood as a sacred way of seeing. The language differs, yet the invitation is constant: notice what is here, allow it to belong, and meet the moment with presence.

Awareness is the quiet space where insight arises, where suffering begins to soften, and where meaning takes root. It is the ground that holds both shadow and light, the inner place where you can turn toward what is difficult and discover that you do not face it alone. In this sense, awareness becomes a spiritual practice not because it requires belief, but because it reveals the deeper currents of your own life.

When you pause long enough to notice a thought, a feeling, or a sensation, you touch something ancient and universal. You join a lineage of people who have chosen to wake up, to look with kindness, and to live with a little more truth. Awareness opens the possibility that transformation is not something you achieve, but something that unfolds when you are willing to be present with what is real.

Reflection

What words or images feel closest to your own sense of awareness as a sacred practice?

How might you honor the quieter dimensions of noticing in your everyday life?

Remember that the invitation to be present is always available, wherever you are, just as you are.

THE SPIRAL OF FORGETTING AND REMEMBERING

Awareness is not a mountain you climb or a badge you earn. It is a spiral, a gentle and living path of returning to yourself again and again. Each moment of forgetting and remembering deepens the groove of self-compassion. Each time you lose your way and notice that you have, you carve a little more space for kindness in your own heart.

You are allowed to be human. You are allowed to wander, to forget, to fall into old stories, and to begin again as many times as you need. With every loop of the spiral, you grow a little softer, a little wiser, and a little freer.

Let this be your quiet encouragement: There is no final arrival. The gift lies in the returning, in the gentle willingness to meet yourself as you are, and in the quiet celebration that arises each time you remember.

Reflection

How does it feel to know that you can always begin again?

Where in your life is the spiral of forgetting and remembering unfolding right now?

Let that possibility meet you, just as you are.

THE GIFT OF AWARENESS

The greatest gift awareness offers is the chance to reclaim agency, dignity, and real presence in your life. Awareness does not promise ease or guarantee that old patterns will vanish quickly. What it does offer is freedom: the freedom to choose, to heal, and to become the person you long to be, again and again.

Each moment of noticing, no matter how brief, is a small act of liberation. With awareness, you remember that you are not only the product of your past or your habits. You are an active participant in your own unfolding, with the power to choose your next step, to forgive yourself, and to begin again as often as needed.

Prompt

What is one thing you have become aware of in your spiral so far?

Is there something you might do differently, or forgive more gently, because of this new awareness?

Let each return be the start of something new, a gentle doorway to freedom and compassion.

AWARENESS AS THE BRIDGE TO TRANSFORMATION

As you move through the spiral of growth, awareness becomes the bridge between your vision, your commitment, and the choices that shape your daily life. Awareness is not a static state. It unfolds moment by moment, a dance between what is seen and unseen, conscious and unconscious.

It is the muscle that helps you sense intuition and resistance, track your nervous system as it moves between safety and activation, and recognize old scripts playing quietly in the background so you can respond rather than repeat them.

Awareness offers the living possibility of choice, again and again. Each pause becomes an opening, an invitation to participate more fully in your own life and to create new pathways for healing and freedom.

AWARENESS IN EVERYDAY LIFE: DEEPENING THE PRACTICE

In the Morning

As you wake, pause before getting out of bed. Notice your first thoughts, sensations, and emotions. Does your mind leap into the day or linger in the softness of morning? Place a hand on your heart and ask, "What wants my attention today?"

Journal Prompt

Write three lines that capture what you notice in body, mind, and spirit. Let the words come naturally.

In the Kitchen

While preparing a meal, pause to feel the textures, notice the scents, and listen to the sounds around you. Are you present, or is your mind wandering? What stories arise about food, care, scarcity, or abundance? Awareness here is not about perfect mindfulness but about simply being with whatever is present.

Prompt

As you eat, notice your urge to speed up, slow down, distract, or savor. How do these urges reflect your emotions or the stories you learned about food and love?

On a Walk

Whether you are in the city or on a quiet trail, let walking become an awareness practice in motion. Feel the rhythm of your steps, the ground beneath your feet, and the play of light and shadow. Notice if you are focused on reaching a destination and experiment with simply being where you are.

Practice

Every so often, pause and look around. What do you notice now that you might have missed? What happens when you move with awareness rather than rushing ahead? Let curiosity guide your steps.

With Technology

Before opening email or scrolling through social media, take a moment to check in. Notice any tension in your shoulders. Do you feel anticipation, dread, or excitement? How do you hold your body as you scroll? What arises in you when you read a message, see a headline, or compare yourself to others?

Awareness Practice

Set a timer for five minutes before or after using technology. Gently notice your sensations, thoughts, and feelings. Name each one as if you are simply saying hello. No judgment is needed. Let this small pause become a soft landing in your day.

Let these simple practices remind you that awareness is not reserved for special moments. It lives in every breath, every ordinary task, and every loop of your spiral. With each return to noticing, you strengthen the bridge between who you have been and who you are becoming.

ADVANCED PRACTICES: THE SPIRAL OF SELF-INQUIRY

At the heart of awareness lies inquiry, an open and compassionate curiosity about your own experience. This practice is not about interrogation or analysis. It is about learning to meet yourself with kindness and a willingness to look beneath the surface, layer by layer.

The Three-Layered Question

Use this practice whenever you notice a strong feeling, reaction, or moment of uncertainty. You can do it aloud, in writing, or as a quiet pause in your day.

Surface: What am I noticing right now?

Tune in to sensation, emotion, or thought. For example, "I feel tightness in my chest," or "I am anxious," or "I am thinking this is too hard."

Story: What story am I telling about this experience?

Notice the narrative that arises. Is it old or new? Is it about you, someone else, or the world? For example, "I always mess things up," "People don't care what I think," or "This feeling means I am failing." Where might this story have begun?

Invitation: What does this moment ask of me?

Without rushing to fix or avoid, ask what this experience might be calling you toward. Is it self-compassion, rest, a boundary, or a new way of seeing? Sometimes the invitation is simply to stay, brethe, and be present.

Practiced regularly, these questions help you spend less time caught in surface reactions and more time connected to the deeper truth beneath them.

Reflection

How might it feel to meet yourself with kindness and curiosity through gentle self-inquiry?

What becomes possible when you ask, listen, and respond instead of reacting?

Let your self-inquiry support your journey home to yourself, one honest moment at a time.

Awareness Journaling: The Spiral Log

Consider keeping a journal devoted to awareness. Each day, you might gently record:

One thing you noticed about yourself

One reaction or trigger and what it reminded you of

One moment of kindness you offered yourself, or wished you had

One intention for the next day ("Tomorrow, I will try to pause before reacting to ...")

Review your entries at the end of each week. Notice patterns: where you tend to react, what softens you, how your intentions shift. Use color, symbols, or simple markings to highlight recurring themes or moments of growth. The act of reviewing reveals how your aware-ness evolves over time, each pass offering a little more clarity and self-understanding.

Awareness and the Unconscious: Inviting the Shadow

Not all awareness is comfortable. Sometimes it reveals the parts of ourselves we would rather keep hidden: anger, envy, grief, longing, or old wounds. Jung called these hidden places the shadow, although every tradition has its own way of naming what is disowned or unwelcomed within.

The invitation is not to fight the shadow or push it aside. It is to meet what arises with curiosity and gentle attention. When we turn toward these exiled parts of ourselves, the possibility for healing and deeper self-understanding begins to open.

Practice: Shadow-Welcoming Script

Sit quietly and bring to mind a recent experience where you felt reactive, ashamed, or unsettled.

Ask yourself, What part of me showed up here? What is it trying to protect or express?

Visualize meeting this part. Give it a color, an age, a shape, or a voice.

Invite it to speak and listen with as much compassion as you can, without correcting or fixing.

Thank this part for its work and ask how it might want to be met next time.

If you wish, journal about what you discovered or draw the shadow as you experienced it. Giving these hidden parts space to be seen softens their intensity and begins to integrate their wisdom into your awareness.

Reflection

What part of your shadow is asking for a little awareness or kindness right now?

How might welcoming these hidden places help you deepen self-acceptance and grow your capacity for compassion?

Remember that the shadow is not an enemy. It is simply a part of you longing to be seen and welcomed home.

THE AWARENESS SPIRAL IN PROFESSIONAL LIFE

Awareness is not only a personal practice. It is foundational in professional life, especially in roles of healing, teaching, and leadership. Bringing awareness into your work keeps your practice honest, responsive, and humble, no matter how seasoned you become.

In Clinical or Coaching Work

Every healing professional knows that awareness is the ground from which transformation grows. Even so, it is easy to slip into routine or autopilot. Returning to presence, again and again, brings freshness and integrity to the work.

Before each session, pause and check in with yourself. What are you bringing into the space? How do you feel physically, emotionally, or energetically?

During a session, track your sensations and internal cues alongside the client's words and emotions. Notice when you feel pulled, resistant, inspired, or distracted.

After a session, reflect with honesty and care. What did you notice about yourself, your reactions, or your impulses? What might you carry forward or approach differently next time?

Even the most experienced clinicians sometimes miss the subtle cues that awareness offers. Making room for reflection keeps your work alive and grounded in intention rather than habit.

In Teaching or Leadership

Awareness is the difference between transactional teaching and transformational learning. It is what opens space for connection, creativity, and shared meaning.

Notice the energy in the room, whether it is a classroom, meeting, or group. Does the space feel open, tense, tired, hopeful, or engaged?

Name what you sense, gently and without judgment. For example, "I am sensing some heaviness today. Does anyone else feel that?" or "There is a lot of energy here right now."

Invite others into the practice. You might begin with a simple check-in, a single word, or a moment of quiet before the work begins.

These small acts of noticing can shift the trajectory of a conversation, a semester, or a project. They create a culture of honesty and shared responsibility for the space you hold together.

Reflection

How might you weave awareness into your professional life, whether as a clinician, teacher, leader, or collaborator?

What changes when you bring curiosity to your experience and invite others to do the same?

Let each return to awareness be a quiet act of leadership, nurturing your growth and the growth of those you serve.

GROUP AND RELATIONSHIP VIGNETTES

The Family Spiral

At a holiday dinner, I watched my niece roll her eyes at a comment from her father. The room tensed a little, old patterns stirring just beneath the surface. My instinct was to smooth things over or change the subject, steering away from the discomfort. Instead, I paused and turned inward, noticing my urge to rescue, the tightening in my chest, and the long family history hanging in the air.

Later, in private, I asked my niece what she had felt in that moment. "It's always like this," she said quietly. "Nobody actually listens." We talked about what it might look like for everyone, not only her, to bring a bit more awareness to these familiar moments.

That year, I introduced a simple check-in before meals: "What is one thing you are feeling right now?" Some family members groaned, others remained silent, and sometimes there were tears. Yet over time, something softened. Even a brief pause before dinner created small ripples, shifting old dynamics and opening space for honesty, tenderness, and healing within the whole family system.

Moments of awareness within families have their own texture, yet the same quiet movement of noticing and returning also unfolds in our work, friendships, and the everyday spaces where we show up with others. Sometimes the spiral appears in far subtler ways, especially when we realize our own ipact.

Awareness and Apology

Not long ago, I said something in a meeting that I later realized had landed poorly. My first instinct was to defend myself, to explain, or to retreat into familiar justifications. Instead, I paused and practiced awareness, noticing the tension in my chest, the urge to run, and the slow rise of shame.

After a night of honest reflection, I chose to apologize. The decision came not from obligation but from an awareness of my impact and a desire to reconnect. The apology was received with relief, and the relationship was strengthened by my willingness to see and own my part.

This is how the spiral often moves in daily life: forgetting, remembering, and gently returning to presence, care, and responsibility.

Reflection

When have you noticed discomfort or conflict in your relationships?

What might shift if you paused for awareness before reacting, fixing, or retreating?

Let these moments remind you that even the smallest touch of awareness can begin to soften and transform the patterns you share with others.

ADVANCED SELF-GUIDED PRACTICES

Awareness does not need long meditations or quiet rooms. Some of the most meaningful changes arise from small rituals woven into daily life. These practices invite you to deepen your spiral, bringing presence and gentle noticing to each step, each transition, and each moment of care.

The Awareness Walk (Guided Script)

Step outside and pause. Stand still, take three slow breaths, and notice your surroundings.

As you begin to walk, focus on the soles of your feet. With each step, silently repeat, "Here. Here. Here."

Whenever your mind wanders, guide your attention back to the step and the word. There is nothing to force and nothing to judge; simply return.

Halfway through your walk, stop for a moment. Look around and notice colors, shapes, and sounds. Tune in to sensations in your body and any shifts in your mood.

Before returning home, place a hand on your heart and offer yourself a quiet thank you for showing up just as you are.

Microawareness Rituals for the Day

Let your day become a tapestry of small, mindful pauses:

At each doorway, pause for a heartbeat and notice your breath.

Before a phone call or meeting, take one conscious breath and ask, "What am I bringing into this moment?"

When eating or drinking, hold the food or mug for a moment and notice its temperature, texture, and aroma before taking a bite or sip.

These micropractices are cumulative. Each small act of noticing anchors you more deeply in awareness, turning even the busiest days into opportunities for presence, kindness, and choice.

Reflection

Which small ritual feels most accessible or nourishing to you right now?

How might these moments of awareness, repeated throughout your day, gently reshape the way you move through life?

Let the spiral of presence meet you in each pause, each step, and each returning breath.

AWARENESS AND HEALING THE PAST

As you move more deeply into awareness, old memories and wounds may resurface. This is not regression or failure. It is a sign that your awareness is opening space for healing at new levels. When echoes from the past arise, you have an opportunity to bring presence and kindness to parts of yourself that once felt alone, unseen, or unloved.

Practice: The Awareness Letter

Choose a younger version of yourself who needs attention or compassion. It might be the child who felt out of place, the young adult facing doubt, or even the version of you who struggled last week.

Write a letter from your present self to that younger self. Name what you notice and what you feel. Offer the words of support you most needed at that time.

When you finish, read the letter aloud and let the words land gently in your heart.

Thank your younger self for finding a way through. Thank your present self for noticing and reaching back with care.

With time, these letters create a bridge between past and present. They make room for healing, self-acceptance, and the deep compassion that supports lasting change.

Reflection

How does it feel to connect with a younger part of yourself in this way?

What message or kindness might you offer that part of you today?

Let your awareness softly weave healing into your story, one letter at a time.

Closing Invitations: Awareness as a Way of Life

Awareness is the soil in which all true growth takes root. It is the portal to authenticity, belonging, and a life aligned with who you really are. There is no finish line and no final exam. There is only the ongoing movement of forgetting and remembering, losing and returning, falling asleep and waking up again.

Let this be your permission slip:

You are allowed to notice without judging.

You are allowed to forget and to remember as many times as you need.

You are allowed to ask for support, to go slowly, and to rest when awareness feels like too much.

Every moment of noticing is an act of self-respect. Every return, no matter how imperfect, is an act of courage. In this gentle coming back to yourself, you deepen the roots of self-acceptance and open the door to new possibility, again and again.

Integration and Stepping Into the Next Spiral

As you close this chapter, take a moment to anchor your awareness:

Name three things you are noticing right now in your body, your heart, and your mind.

Thank yourself for being willing to notice, even when it feels uncomfortable or unclear.

Set a gentle intention: "May I meet myself with kindness and return to awareness whenever I am ready."

The next chapter, "Living Into Your Intention," builds on everything you have explored here. It will guide you from inner awareness into embodied, real-world change. Your spiral continues, made richer and wiser by every moment of seeing, naming, and allowing.

Final Spiral Prompts

What is one area of your life where you most want to deepen awareness?

*What does awareness feel like in your body and in your rela-
tionships?*

What old story is ready to be seen, named, or gently rewritten?

*What is your commitment today to awareness as a soft, ongoing
practice rather than perfection?*

*Let your answers become a quiet celebration of how far you have
come and a blessing for all the returning still ahead.*

Transition

As you step forward, remember that each spiral of awareness
lays the foundation for the next. In the coming chapter, you'll
be invited to live into your intention, bringing all that you
have seen and named into real, embodied action. May you
meet yourself, again and again, with kindness, courage, and
the freedom that only awareness can bring.

8. LIVING INTO YOUR INTENTION: STEP 4 OF THE 5-POINT PROCESS

The journey between who you once were, and who you are becoming, is where the dance of life really takes place.

— BARBARA DE ANGELIS

FROM INTENTION TO ACTION: THE ALCHEMY OF BECOMING

THERE COMES A MOMENT, sometimes so quiet it might go unnoticed, when what you've longed for begins to stir beneath the surface, looking for a way to become real. You've named your intention and you've tended it, gently, as one tends a seed or a dream at dawn. Now, like water that has gathered strength deep within the earth, your intention seeks a path out into the open air, sometimes in a rush, more often in slow, persistent currents.

You may find that the shift from longing to living has less to do with bold declarations and more to do with the subtle work of allowing: a choice here, a pause there, a new way of noticing what is already present. This is the alchemy of becoming, a river shaping stone not by force but through gentle and unrelenting presence. Every small act, and every return after forgetting, becomes another ripple that is quiet and patient yet powerful enough to carve canyons over time.

Some days, it might feel like nothing is changing at all. Yet beneath the surface, old patterns are being smoothed, new pathways opening, the future rearranging itself, just as a river finds its way forward even when the land seems unmoving.

THE INVITATION TO UNFOLDING

You might pause here, even for a breath, and notice how it feels to let yourself not know, to simply follow the gentle flow of what wants to unfold next? Each section that follows is another bend in the river. You're invited to explore, to linger, to allow whatever meaning emerges, knowing that, in this work, the journey is always as important as any destination.

THE TRANSFORMATIVE POWER OF *ACT AS IF*

Sometimes, the most profound changes begin not with certainty but with the smallest willingness to experiment. Imagine, just for a moment, what might happen if you allowed yourself to move in the world as if what you long for is already quietly unfolding. You may not need to know how, or even believe it fully. It's enough to set the scene, to step onto the stage of your own life and let yourself rehearse a new way of being: one breath, one glance, one word at a time.

Throughout history and across traditions, this simple practice has woven its way through the work of healers, philosophers, and mystics. Gestalt therapists invite you to act as if, not because you're pretending but because every act is a rehearsal, an experiment, a gentle opening to new feelings and possibilities. Alfred Adler called on us to behave as if we are already the people we hope to become, knowing that each small act changes the script. Spiritual teachers, too, have offered this wisdom: Pray as if you have already received. Assume the feeling of the wish fulfilled. Act as if you already are, and notice how the universe finds you.

Why does this work? Not because we deny the present or try to leap over our doubts but because the body and the mind are always listening, always learning. When you act as if, you invite your nervous system and imagination to join you in a gentle rehearsal. Neuroscience tells us that the brain cannot easily tell the difference between vividly imagined experience and reality. Each experiment in living, each small gesture, quietly builds new pathways, possibility becoming practice, practice becoming change.

You might discover, too, that acting as if takes the pressure off. It isn't about perfection or performance. It's play, a freedom to discover, to test, to surprise yourself with what might actually fit. Sometimes just stepping into the energy of your future self, even for a moment, is enough to shift the entire day.

So as you move into this practice, let it be gentle. Let yourself play at the edges of who you are and who you're becoming. Notice what happens when you act as if the change you seek is already possible, because in many ways that is where true transformation begins.

ADVANCED NEUROSCIENCE:
EMBODYING THE CHANGE

It's a quiet marvel, really, how the body and mind are always learning, always listening, even when we think nothing is happening. Modern neuroscience tells us what ancient wisdom has always hinted: When you allow yourself to act as if, you do more than simply imagine a new way of being. You begin to invite your very biology to join you in the experiment.

With each small step, an intention embodied, a vision rehearsed in the mind's eye, you gently shape the wiring of your own brain. This is neuroplasticity at work: the brain's lifelong gift for adaptation, for forming new pathways in response to practice and belief, no matter how many times you've circled the old.

Olympic athletes know this. Before they ever leap or sprint, they close their eyes and feel every detail of the race, the surge of energy, the rhythm of breath, the stretch and release of muscle. Science has shown their brains firing as if the race itself is already being run. And so it is in daily life. When you take time to picture yourself living your intention, when you let a microaction give that vision a home in your body, you're sending a signal: This is who I am becoming. Each small gesture is both rehearsal and reality, teaching the mind and the muscles that a new pattern is possible.

I have seen this in my own unfolding. Years before earning my doctorate, I set my intention in motion with a single license plate, PHDBOUND. Each time I glimpsed it, something inside grew a little more familiar with the idea of becoming. Before my move to México, I lived into the energy of belonging and new possibility, sometimes in my kitchen, sometimes just in a quiet moment of breath. Even writing this book, I began with a ritual: crafting a mock cover, giving form to the yet-unwritten dream. What seemed like small gestures were, in truth, the daily touchstones that allowed intention to step forward and take its place in the real.

If the brain loves what is repeated, then consistency is your most loyal companion. The awkwardness of first steps is a sign you're walking a new path. Every time you show up for your intention, even in the smallest way, you strengthen a new connection. Over time, what felt unfamiliar becomes the new home ground.

Research affirms this: Lasting change does not depend on a single burst of effort but on the quiet devotion of return. Daily practice, paired with honest reflection, teaches your mind and your world to recognize and welcome the new reality you are growing. Even as you read these words, some part of you may be preparing to practice in ways you won't yet notice, and that's just fine.

You might imagine your new intention as a young root, quietly searching for water beneath the surface. With each repetition, each small action, each return, you nourish this root, helping it to find its way, to strengthen and anchor, until one day you look back and realize that the landscape has changed. The river has carved a new path. And you are living into a life shaped not just by dreams but by the steady, natural work of becoming.

MY STORY: REHEARSING THE FUTURE

Before a single suitcase was packed, long before a plane ticket was booked, my journey to México began as most journeys do, in small, ordinary moments that quietly reimagined the familiar. In Santa Fe, I let myself be guided not by sudden declarations but by the soft gravity of daily ritual. There, in my kitchen, a handful of chiles or a splash of lime in a glass became more than flavor, they became gentle reminders of where I was heading, as if I were already greeting the sun in another country.

It was not always graceful. My Spanish came out in starts and stops, awkward and uncertain, echoing off the walls as I rehearsed verbs and stumbled through conversations with myself. The bills I paid still carried the old currency, but in my mind pesos began to appear where dollars used to live. It sometimes felt as though I was simply pretending. At other times, a deeper part of me already belonged.

With each small decision––what to keep, what to give away, how to arrange the colors on my table or the hours of my day––I allowed the future to arrive in pieces, quietly making room for a self not yet fully known. None of this was grand. No fireworks, no moment of final arrival. Only a quiet, persistent willingness to let tomorrow's self borrow today's habits, as if rehearsal itself was an act of becoming.

There is a kind of magic that emerges when you allow yourself to live into your vision even before it feels real. The world, it seems, notices your commitment. A friend offers unexpected help. A door opens where none was visible before. The unknown grows less intimidating; your own courage becomes less a wish and more a companion at your side.

If you are wondering how to begin, let this story be a gentle nudge. Living into alignment rarely announces itself with clarity or certainty. It is more often a series of small permissions: to cook as if you belong, to speak words not yet fluent, to set a place at the table for a new chapter. Each act, no matter how unremarkable it seems, invites the future to take root in the present.

You do not need to leap all at once. Let your own rehearsal be quiet, sometimes awkward, sometimes beautifully right. It is enough to let your longing inform a gesture, a sentence, a choice. Trust that with each return you are shaping your days into something new, step by imperfect step.

And so, as you stand at the threshold of your own becoming, you might notice that the journey is already underway, carried on the gentle current of your willingness to begin. The world, as always, is waiting for your next quiet rehearsal.

Perhaps even now you can pause just for a breath and wonder what small act, what tiny rehearsal, might invite your own future a bit closer, starting today.

THE PRACTICE OF ACT AS IF IN EVERYDAY LIFE

There's a quiet, transformative power in the practice of acting as if. Not pretending, not forcing, and certainly not denying your doubts, just allowing yourself to embody the confidence or courage your vision calls for, even if just for a moment. Acting as if is less about certainty and more about willingness. It means beginning where you are, trusting that belief and momentum will gather as you go, like mist collecting over a river at dawn.

Often, you don't wait to feel ready or even convinced. Instead, you make a small shift such as a posture, a word, a choice, each one a pebble dropped gently into the current, sending ripples in directions you can't yet see. This is how new stories are written, quietly disrupting the old narratives of "not yet," "not me," "not possible." You step, one act at a time, into a new possibility, letting the old scripts loosen their hold.

I remember how this practice met me in moments of doubt, especially when I longed for change in the patterns of health and self-care. At first, each new choice felt strange, almost like an impersonation. Some part of me doubted I truly deserved nourishment, rest, or kindness. So I made a quiet agreement with myself: Just act as if I do, even if only for five minutes. I sat down to a meal, walked outside, or let myself pause, even while the old doubts whispered in the background. Gradually, my actions began to shape my sense of self until belief, too, found its way home.

This practice became a thread I could follow, especially on days when confidence or energy faltered. I learned not to demand transformation all at once but to recommit to just one as-if for that day: a sunny chair, a cup of tea, a more loving response to an email. Small acts, easy to overlook, yet each one a seed quietly rooting the future in the present. Over time, these moments of willingness stacked up, almost unnoticeable at first, but ultimately more powerful than any grand burst of effort.

To act as if is not to delude yourself. It's an invitation to let the next version of you enter the room and take a seat, even before you feel fully ready. With each choice, you rehearse the life you want until rehearsal and reality begin to blend. The world doesn't need your perfection; it asks only for your participation, your willingness to try, and the courage to embody change, one authentic act at a time.

Sometimes, I smile at how this has circled back in my own life. I once dreamed of being an actor, stepping into stories on stage for an audience. Now, acting as if has become something different, not performance but devotion. Each day, I write the script for the person I am becoming, one gesture, one line, one hope at a time. In our own way, we are all actors in the great unfolding, a rehearsal not for others but for the lives and selves we most long to inhabit.

Perhaps, as you read, you'll notice a small *as if* of your own, waiting patiently to be tried just once, and then again.

LIVING THE PRACTICE: HOW TO ACT AS IF EVERY DAY

What if, instead of searching for the right way to begin, you simply noticed where the impulse to become is already nudging at you? Perhaps there's a part of your life that calls softly for renewal, a role you're longing to step into, a habit ready to be transformed, or just a single moment in the day that wants to feel more aligned.

You might start by letting a question linger: How would I act, right now, if this were already true? You don't need to have all the answers. Instead, you can let your imagination try on small details, such as what you would wear, how you would speak, what you might say yes or no to, and how you would move through your day if you trusted that you belonged in this new story.

There is no need for grand gestures. You can let the practice be as small as a breath, a meal, a single sentence. Perhaps you write a page before coffee or cook a meal that reminds you of where you're going. Perhaps you speak a new language imperfectly (as I still do!) or allow yourself to be new and awkward and alive. Every misstep is proof you are in motion; every stumble is a sign that you are learning to walk a new path.

You might anchor the feeling in a journal, a few words about what's different or what resistance and excitement show up when you take a small risk. You could ask yourself what kind of support would help you stay with the experiment a bit longer. Let the page hold your discoveries and watch how the smallest acts become the most meaningful evidence over time.

Sometimes the feeling catches up with the action, sometimes not. Either way, each small rehearsal builds a little more faith, first in your body, then in your spirit, then in the shape of your days. You might also notice that celebration has a quiet power. Even the smallest win, noticed and honored, can teach your heart that you are becoming someone new.

So take a breath, and let today's as if be gentle, imperfect, real. Trust that you are practicing a life that fits, one ordinary moment at a time.

Prompt

You might pause here and let your pen wander across the page:

What's one small as if you could practice today?

How would it feel to allow yourself to try it on and see what grows, even if for a few moments?

ACTING AS IF IN EVERYDAY LIFE: CLIENT AND STUDENT SNAPSHOTS

Change sometimes announces itself in quiet ways. You might notice it in a new shirt, a different tone in your voice, or the way you reach for something just beyond your usual grasp.

These stories are like stones in a stream, distinct yet smoothed by the same current of willingness.

Lisa, for instance, wanted to feel more confident at work. Rather than wait for certainty, she began dressing as if she already held the position she imagined for herself. Even before any promotion, she let her presence do the talking, voicing ideas with a bit more assurance. Over time, her posture shifted. Her colleagues took notice. Something real yet intangible began to settle in and take root. The environment changed around her, just as she was changing within.

Luis dreamed of being a musician. Long before any gigs were booked, he started to live as if he was already a working artist, practicing, seeking out local musicians, even introducing himself in this new way. It wasn't an overnight success, but with each small as if, the world seemed to listen. One year later, he was performing regularly, and what began as an experiment had quietly become his reality.

Then there's Brenda, who was learning to trust herself in anxious moments. Rather than waiting for all the fear to dissolve, she began with the smallest acts, meeting someone's eyes, saying hello, taking note of her own quiet strengths. The world didn't transform overnight, but her courage grew with each brave step. New possibilities began to gather at the edges of her days, just within reach.

You may find your own story weaving in and out of these vignettes, a reminder that acting as if is less about pretending and more about giving your next self a gentle invitation to come forward, in small, steady ways.

THE MESSY MIDDLE: EMBRACING UNCERTAINTY

Between the spark of intention and the ease that sometimes comes with mastery, there is a space I've come to call the "messy middle." This is the land of awkwardness, uncertainty, and self-doubt, a liminal place where you may not see results yet and where old patterns, with all their comfort, call you back. Most of us, when we find ourselves here, want to hurry through or escape altogether. Yet it's here, in this tender territory, that the deepest roots of transformation quietly find their grip.

If you traveled with me through the first *A Life Aligned*, you might recognize this as the "neutral zone," a kind of twilight where the old way has crumbled and the new way has yet to fully take form. The neutral zone can feel lonely, even frightening. You might wonder if you're lost, if you'll ever "arrive." Yet this uncertainty is not an absence but a womb. It's sacred ground, a threshold where what was and what will be are both held in the dark, fertile silence.

Think of a seed, nestled in soil. At first, there is only darkness and the slow, silent work of rooting. Nothing visible above the surface, no sign of change for the outside world. But deep down life is busy, tiny roots testing the earth, seeking nourishment, anchoring in unseen ways. If you find yourself in this messy middle, know that your own roots are taking hold, quietly preparing for what will come.

You are not broken or failing if you find yourself here. Quite the opposite. The messy middle is proof that you are in motion, stretching, growing, and gently pushing past your former edges. Yes, there may be darkness. Yes, there may be loneliness. But there is hope too, a quiet hope that lives in every moment you show up, even when it feels uncomfortable. To linger here, even for a single breath, is an act of faith in your own unfolding.

Stay with the process. Let yourself trust the neutral zone. In this darkness, seeds are sprouting. In the silence, your new self is quietly taking root.

Vignette: Navigating the Messy Middle

Samantha, a teacher stepping into a new career, felt a rush of inspiration at first. But as the new path revealed its bumps and detours, fear took hold. "I kept thinking I should feel more confident by now," she wrote in her journal. Together, we explored: Could each mistake be a sign she was learning, not failing? Over time, Samantha began to see that the awkwardness, the discomfort, was not a verdict but a sign of movement, a sign that she was on her way.

Prompt

You might pause to wonder:

What is a messy middle moment in your own life, right now or in the past?

What did you learn in the shadows?

What can you quietly celebrate about your willingness to keep moving, even when you couldn't see the way?

This is the place where your resilience, your humor, and your adaptability are slowly built. Here you discover that your worth is not measured by getting everything right but by the gentle faithfulness of returning to your intention, again and again, even when the path is unclear. Remember, roots deepen in the dark, and new life is being prepared where you cannot yet see.

TROUBLESHOOTING: WHEN LIVING INTO FEELS HARD

There are times on this path when living into your intention feels anything but graceful. If you find yourself resisting, comparing, stumbling, or simply weary, you are not alone. These are natural eddies along the river, familiar to anyone walking the spiral of growth.

When resistance appears, it's only human to want to retreat to the comfort of what's known. Rather than pushing it away, you might pause and gently ask, What is this feeling trying to protect? Resistance is often a quiet guardian, a part of you longing for safety. Offer yourself compassion here and allow the next step to be small, sometimes as simple as a breath, a softening, a whisper of willingness.

Comparison, too, may arise. Watching others seem to move faster or further can bring envy or a sting of shame. But the truth is, every journey unfolds in its own season. You can return, again and again, to your own intention, your unique story, your quietly emerging values. The river does not rush to the sea by following another's current.

Setbacks are inevitable. When you slip or lose your way, what would it be like to meet yourself with gentle curiosity instead of blame? Each misstep carries a lesson. Growth is never linear. The spiral leads us back, not to the same place but to a new vantage, a deeper understanding.

And when exhaustion or burnout signals the need to rest, remember: Living into your intention is not a test of endurance. The dance includes pauses, stillness, and moments of reflection. Sometimes the most aligned act is to set everything down for a time, to breathe, and to let yourself be gathered by rest.

Living into is a practice, not a standard you must measure up to. When you falter, your only job is to begin again, one breath, one step, one small kindness at a time. Each return is a triumph, and each moment of compassion is a quiet, essential part of the journey.

LIVING INTO INTENTION IN RELATIONSHIP AND COMMUNITY

There's a quiet magic that happens when living into intention becomes a shared experience. What might feel daunting alone can become lighter, even joyful, when witnessed by others who hold space for your growth. Sometimes, all it takes is the presence of a trusted friend, a partner, or a circle, those who see you not only as you are but as you are becoming.

You might invite others into your process to share a goal, ask for gentle accountability, or simply celebrate each small win together. In these moments, your intention takes on new energy, a chorus, not a solo. Consider joining a group or community where the language of growth and becoming is spoken, where each person's unfolding is valued.

Vignette: Mutual Support

Roberto and Elena, friends separated by miles, set intentions together at the start of each month, their faces meeting over video call. Each week, they exchange simple texts, small updates, quiet encouragement. "It's not about perfect progress," Elena reminds, "It's about having someone who remembers what you're trying to become and who believes in you on the days you forget." In this way, even across distance, intention is woven with gentle threads of companionship.

Within community, you discover a tapestry richer than your own single thread. Witnessing others' journeys, watching their struggles, celebrating their wins, you see that your challenges are not personal flaws but shared human experiences. Your own acts, no matter how small, ripple outward, coloring the larger design.

INCLUSION, JUSTICE, AND LIVING INTO INTENTION TOGETHER

No journey unfolds in isolation. Each time you live into your intention, you plant a seed that may take root in unexpected places, changing not only your life but the world around you. Small acts such as offering kindness, setting a boundary, or daring to speak up can shift the atmosphere of a room, a workplace, or a community.

Social justice, healing, and true transformation begin with individuals willing to practice new ways of being, even when the world feels resistant or slow to change. Your courage can become permission for others, especially in spaces where your voice or perspective has not always been seen or heard.

Vignette: Community Intention

Manuel and his friends longed for a more welcoming city. Together, they held the intention to act as if everyone belongs. It started simply: monthly potlucks, reaching out to newcomers, eventually growing into an advocacy group. Each gesture was small, but over time these acts wove a new story of inclusion, one where each person could imagine themselves at home.

When you practice living into your intention, especially when you feel alone or underrepresented, you become a quiet kind of leader. You make it easier for the next person to try, to risk, to believe. Your intention, lived out, ripples into places you may never see yet always matter.

ADVANCED EMBODIMENT: BRINGING INTENTION INTO THE BODY

Living into intention is not a mental act alone. The body is the landscape where change quietly takes root. Sometimes the subtlest shift, a deepening of breath, a change in posture, a gentle touch, becomes the place where intention finds its way from idea into reality.

If confidence calls to you, perhaps you notice what it feels like to let your feet ground you a little more, to let your spine lengthen or your gaze lift. If compassion is your aim, you might tune in to the softness of your jaw, the warmth in your chest, the way your hands move when speaking gently to yourself or another. Every body is different; every intention a unique dance.

With time, these physical anchors become quiet companions. A gesture, a movement, or a single breath can serve as a gentle way to act as if, even before your mind has caught up. The body remembers what the heart longs for, and repetition turns intention from idea into living truth.

You might even pause now and notice: Is there a gesture, a posture, a way of moving that wants to express your intention in this moment? Let it be small, easy, even playful. Over time, such anchors become second nature, quietly shaping who you are becoming.

RITUALS, MICROACTIONS, AND REPETITION: ANCHORING CHANGE

Big change is less a single leap than a mosaic of countless small actions, strung like pearls across the ordinary days. You might start by writing your intention in your journal each morning or whispering it into the quiet. Sometimes saying it aloud or feeling it settle in your body brings it to life in unexpected ways.

Throughout the day, the practice continues, tiny, almost invisible microactions. Maybe it's placing a gentle hand on your heart before answering an email, taking a five-minute pause when tension arises, or arranging a small stone or note somewhere you'll see it. Each act, though small, calls you back to yourself.

In the evening, as the day unwinds, you might reflect: How did I live into my intention today? Where did I drift? What small celebration can I offer for even the tiniest step forward? The repetition of these rituals and microactions weaves a thread through your days, infusing them with meaning, confidence, and a quiet hope that grows with every return.

You may discover that change is not something you force but something you plant and tend, moment by moment, breath by breath, allowing each small act to become a seed of the life you are growing.

MY STORY: LIVING INTO DISCOMFORT AND FINDING NEW STRENGTH

During my transition to life in México, living into intention became more than believing in change; it became a willingness to dwell inside uncertainty, in what I have come to know as the neutral zone. It is that shadowy, in-between space where the old has quietly slipped away but the new has not yet found its form. Every day was a walk through unfamiliar territory: speaking Spanish while often unsure of the right word, navigating unfamiliar paperwork, learning how to ask for help, even with the simplest things.

Some days, the neutral zone felt dark and echoing, familiar routines dissolving, self-doubt speaking loudly in the silence. I found comfort in simplicity. On those days, my only intention might be: Today, I will allow myself to feel uncomfortable, knowing this is part of growth. On other days: Today, I will celebrate one small victory, however minor it seems.

In this messy middle, discomfort was not failure but a signpost, a necessary rite of passage. Each awkward conversation, each moment of confusion became an invitation to trust that the unknown was quietly fertile, preparing the ground for something new.

What still surprises me is how the spiral always returns. Even now, as I revise these words, offering new language for old lessons, I sometimes find myself back in the neutral zone. Anxiety, doubt, questions about "getting it right" rise up as faithful companions. I've come to see this not as regression but as the spiral in motion, circling through familiar fears and emerging possibilities, again and again.

Over time, small choices, acts of faith, self-compassion, and the willingness to return, begin to accumulate, transforming fear into confidence, discomfort into a sense of belonging. On days I feel lost or unsure of progress, coming back to intention, even for a few breaths, restores a sense of purpose and agency.

If you find yourself in this place, between what was and what is not yet, know that you are not alone. And you are not lost. With every uncertain step, you become a little more at home in the world around you, and, perhaps more importantly, in yourself. This is the hidden gift of the messy middle: In choosing to stay, you discover strength and new possibility that simply cannot be found on familiar ground.

HONORING RESISTANCE AND CELEBRATING RETURN

If resistance rises up, you might greet it as a messenger, not an enemy. Sometimes it points to places that need a bit more care, gentleness, or even just a pause. Other times, resistance is the subtle signal that an old identity is ready to loosen its grip. In either case, what matters most is your willingness to return to your intention, your ritual, your why. That act of coming back, no matter how many detours you've taken, is itself a quiet triumph.

When resistance appears, you might find it helpful to pause and wonder, What is my resistance trying to teach me right now? Perhaps you let your pen wander, letting the answer find you on the page. You may be surprised by what emerges, and the way forward may gently reveal itself in time.

As you move through the spiral, remember to celebrate every return. The most powerful journeys are not those that follow a straight path but those that are marked by the courage to begin again and again.

SELF-COMPASSION AND THE POWER OF RETURN

No journey ever unfolds in a perfect line. There will be days you forget, resist, or feel lost. Your task is not to be flawless but simply to keep returning. Each return, each time you notice, soften, and choose to begin again, is a victory, a living sign of your willingness to grow.

Self-Compassion Practice

You might offer yourself the kindness you'd give a beloved friend. When you slip, pause and remind yourself: It's okay to be human. I can begin again right now.

In the spiral of living into intention, every return is a renewal. The more gently you can meet yourself, the more space you create for genuine, lasting change.

THE BODY, THE NERVOUS SYSTEM, AND LIVING INTO

The nervous system is a creature of habit. It gravitates toward what is familiar even when that familiarity no longer serves your deeper longing. In many ways, living into your intention is an act of loving re-education, a quiet invitation to gently stretch your comfort zone and then retreat and rest when needed. Over time, with patience and practice, what once felt new and awkward can become a place of ease, a natural home in your body.

You might find it helpful to notice, week by week, where in your body you feel on track or off track. Let your journal hold your discoveries about sensation, tension, or openness. Use your breath or a simple movement to gently recalibrate.

These small acts of somatic awareness are the bridge between intention and embodiment, a spiral path of becoming at the most basic, cellular level.

Somatic Exercise

Pause for a moment and bring your attention to your body, just as it is. Notice where you feel grounded and where you feel tense or unsettled.

Now, let your breath move slowly and easily, as if you are inviting space into any area of tightness.

If you wish, place a gentle hand on your heart, your belly, or wherever you sense your intention lives today.

With each inhale, imagine nourishment arriving. With each exhale, let something soften.

You might stay here for a few breaths, allowing sensation and intention to meet. No need to force, just notice what shifts, if anything.

When you're ready, gently open your eyes or lift your gaze, bringing a bit more of your intention into this moment.

LIVING INTO INTENTION WHEN THE WORLD FEELS HEAVY

There will be days when the outside world feels heavy, when illness, loss, injustice, or unexpected change threaten to pull you away from your intention. In these moments, your practice may need to become very simple: perhaps just a breath, a single kind word to yourself, or the willingness to keep going, even if only barely.

Honor this. Even in the hardest seasons, the willingness to return––to your intention, to your breath, to a single point of light––is enough. Alignment is not measured by how much you accomplish but by your ability to honor your own limits with gentleness.

Prompt

You might pause and ask yourself: What is the smallest way I can live into my intention today, no matter what else is happening? Sometimes simply pausing, breathing, and offering yourself a measure of kindness is the truest act of living into your intention.

Advanced Storytelling: New Narratives in Action

Living into intention is also a practice of story, of noticing the old narratives that quietly shape your days and then, with care, choosing to tell a new story. If you've always carried the belief, "I give up too easily," what would happen if you remembered a time, maybe even just a moment, when you persisted? If your story has been one of not belonging, what shifts if you recall a time you found your place, however briefly?

Your journal can become a garden for these new stories. Each week you might write a few lines about a win, a time, big or small, when you lived into your intention. Let these stories be gentle anchors, rooting your new reality in something lived and real.

Practice

Each week, write a short story about a moment you lived into your intention.

Allow these stories to become seeds for the life you're growing.

CLIENT AND STUDENT STORIES: COURAGE IN THE EVERYDAY

Sometimes, the most courageous acts are the smallest ones, quiet shifts that change everything over time.

DeShawn's New Boundaries

DeShawn had spent a lifetime putting others first. When he set the intention to honor his own needs, it wasn't dramatic or loud. It was a string of small acts: declining an extra project, asking for help when overwhelmed, permitting himself to rest. At first, he worried that these choices would seem selfish. But with each gentle no, DeShawn noticed more energy, more joy, and, perhaps most beautifully, a deeper connection with those around him. What began as a boundary became a gift, a living example that others could follow.

Maria's Act As If

Maria, the first in her family to pursue a doctorate, felt the weight of imposter syndrome in every classroom and meeting. Her intention was to show up with presence even when she felt she didn't belong. So she practiced acting as if she was meant to be there, asking questions, mentoring other students, slowly finding her own voice. With time, her act became her reality, and she became a source of hope and strength for others following her path.

Elliot's Return to Joy

Elliot arrived in coaching after a long season of burnout. His intention was simple: to reconnect with joy in his work and daily life. This meant trying new things, taking walks at lunch, building playlists that made him smile, bringing humor to tense meetings. When joy felt distant, he tracked small sparks in his journal. Over time, what began as effort became a new way of being. Joy, once a stranger, became a regular guest.

As you read these stories, you might notice a thread connecting them to your own life, the possibility that, in even the smallest choices, your story can shift. Sometimes it starts not with the ending in mind but simply with the willingness to try.

AWE, AGENCY, AND BELONGING: THE GIFTS OF LIVING INTO

As you live into your intention, you may begin to notice quiet, unexpected gifts taking shape, a sense of agency blooming as you realize you can choose your way forward, a new belonging as you settle more deeply into your own life, moments of awe as small changes slowly become real transformation. Celebrate these gifts however quietly they arrive. They are living proof of your capacity to evolve, to shape a life that is aligned with your deepest truth.

Awe Practice

Each day, let yourself notice one thing, however small, that is beautiful or meaningful: the color of a sunrise, the curve of a smile, the feeling of a small victory. Perhaps you record it in your journal or simply let awe be your silent companion as you move through the day.

Exercise: Living Into Your Intention

Over the next week, you might choose a single intention you wish to embody.

Each morning, write it gently in your journal. Each evening, reflect on how you lived into it. What worked? What didn't? What surprised you? Notice the small wins, the subtle shifts, the places where change feels possible.

At week's end, write a letter to yourself. Celebrate your progress, your effort, and your willingness to try, even when the path was not clear.

Advanced Practice: Living Into Intention in Challenging Times

There will be seasons when living into intention feels heavy or nearly impossible. The world may ask more than you have to give. Uncertainty, illness, loss, or simply the weight of daily life may slow you down. In these times, let your intention become very simple. Perhaps it is only to survive, to rest, to breathe, or to offer yourself the smallest moment of kindness. Trust that this is enough.

Resilience Exercise:

When things are hard, let yourself anchor in the smallest possible step. If all you can do is rest, name it. Honor it. Allow yourself to return when you are able, knowing that every return, no matter how small, is a quiet act of courage.

INCLUSION AND COLLECTIVE LIVING INTO

Your journey, though uniquely your own, never unfolds in isolation. Each time you live into your intention, you quietly open doors for others. A student may notice your courage and find a bit more bravery in themselves. A colleague, moved by your honesty, may discover new permission to be real. A family member might glimpse your joy and remember their own longing to step forward.

In this way, your actions ripple outward, sometimes in ways you'll never see. You become a participant in something larger, each step you take planting seeds of possibility in the soil of community.

Collective Prompt

You might wonder, just for a moment: How could your willingness to live into intention create new possibilities for your family, your workplace, your community? Each small act is a beginning. Your progress paves the way for others. Every return is a seed for collective transformation.

FINAL REFLECTIONS: THE ONGOING DANCE

Living into intention is not a single achievement or a box to check. It is a lifelong process: a spiral, a dance of courage, humility, and endless return. There will always be new edges, fresh invitations, and challenges that call you to act as if all over again. Some days the steps feel graceful. Other days, awkward or uncertain. This, too, is the rhythm of true growth.

There is no perfect; there is only practice. Each time you show up for your intention, no matter how small, no matter how uncertain, you are not just creating a new story for yourself but also quietly changing the world around you. With every act of courage, every moment of humility, every choice to begin again, you send ripples out into your family, your community, and the larger world.

Let awe, compassion, and celebration be your constant companions. Honor your smallest wins. Offer yourself grace when you falter. Remember, you are never alone in this spiral. Every soul who dares to live with intention is a fellow dancer on the path.

The world aches for the story you are living into, one imperfect, beautiful step at a time. Your willingness to keep dancing, to keep choosing, to keep returning, is a gift both to yourself and to a world hungry for authenticity and hope.

A BLESSING FOR LIVING INTO YOUR INTENTION

May you find the courage to step forward, even when the path is uncertain and your heart beats loudly in your chest.

May you discover comfort in the messy middle, trusting that
every awkward step is itself an act of hope.

May awe find you in small, ordinary moments: a shaft of
sunlight, a burst of laughter, the sound of your own voice
daring to speak what is true.

May compassion be the hand you extend to yourself when
you stumble and celebration the way you honor each return.

May you remember that you are never alone, that your
journey sends quiet ripples far beyond what you can see.

And may the universe meet your devotion with
opportunities, companions, and unexpected grace, catching
you as you leap, again and again.

Living into your intention is where you begin to author your
aligned life. The final step is integration, gathering your
growth, your insights, and the habits you have nurtured,
until alignment is no longer just a practice but a way of
being. Next, we'll explore what it means to truly live a life
aligned and how to sustain your progress through all of life's
inevitable changes.

9. INTEGRATION: STEP 5 OF THE 5-POINT PROCESS

We do not learn from experience ... we learn from reflecting on experience.

— JOHN DEWEY

WHAT IS INTEGRATION?

IF YOU JOURNEYED with me through the original *A Life Aligned*, you may recall that this chapter once bore a different name, "Living a Life Aligned." That fit the spirit of the work at the time, celebrating the sense of having arrived at the life you set out to create. But the deeper I traveled into my own unfolding, and the more I listened to the stories of those I work with, I began to see that true alignment is never a final destination. It's a living, ongoing process, one that spirals back upon itself, gathering meaning with each return. That's why the focus is on integration in this evolved edition.

Integration is both art and science, a weaving together of every lesson, every experience, every part of yourself, until what was once scattered begins to form a living, breathing tapestry. Integration is both the culmination of your journey and the gentle threshold of a new way of being. It's where your many threads, what you know, what you feel, what you long for, begin to move in harmony.

In psychology, integration is the process of bringing together all parts of the self so you can move through life with coherence and authenticity. In healing traditions, it is a return to center, a remembering of what has been scattered or set aside, and a welcoming back of what once felt disconnected. In daily life, integration becomes the quiet sense of being at home with yourself, even as you continue to grow.

Integration is not the absence of struggle or contradiction. It means holding complexity with a wide embrace, making space for dreams and doubts, past and possibility, wounds and wisdom, all within the same field of compassionate awareness. To be integrated is not to erase any part of yourself but instead to invite each part to the table, trusting that every voice belongs and that every piece has a role in your wholeness.

True integration is less about arrival and more about flow, a deep, ongoing sense that whatever arises, joy or grief, clarity or confusion, you can witness, respond, and adjust, rooted in who you have become. Integration is how your growth becomes embodied and how your wisdom is made real, not just for you but for those whose lives you touch.

This, then, is why this chapter and this process have evolved. Living a life aligned is not about holding on to a perfect, fixed state. It's about embodying your alignment, moment by moment, in a world that is always changing. Integration is the art of making your transformation sustainable, resilient, and truly your own.

INTEGRATION AS ONGOING SELF-DISCOVERY

Integration is never truly done. It is a lifelong spiral, a continual unfolding and gentle reweaving, as each season of life reveals new dimensions of who you are. Every fresh chapter––moving to a new place, beginning or ending a relationship, shifting careers, facing loss or illness––invites parts of you into the light that you may not have seen before. What once felt seamless or whole may be shaken, surprised, or stretched by change. This isn't regression; it's life inviting you into deeper and deeper wholeness.

Integration is the art of meeting yourself exactly where you are, again and again, with honesty, kindness, and curiosity. Sometimes the path will introduce you to parts of yourself that have been quiet until now. Sometimes you'll revisit old patterns but at a new depth, with gentler eyes and more refined tools. Integration is not a finish line but a living practice, a willingness to welcome each new version of yourself home, again and again, as the spiral continues.

Vignette: The Unexpected Return

Ann had worked hard, made real progress, and was proud of her growth. Then old anxieties rushed back in after becoming a parent. Her old coping tools seemed to falter, and with them came the shameful whisper: "Shouldn't I be past this by now?" But with gentle support, Ann discovered that parenting had surfaced pieces of herself she'd never met––hidden fears, hopes, and ancient family stories that wanted a voice. Integration for Ann became about welcoming these "new old" parts, drawing on her experience while inventing new rituals. She found that true wholeness means letting every part have its say, even the ones that surprise you, and even the ones that arrive late.

Integration is ongoing self-discovery, a humility to meet yourself anew, the courage to revise your story, and the grace to include every piece, spiraling ever deeper into alignment.

Integration in Real Life

Integration is not a dramatic moment or a single break-through. It is found in the small, invisible choices that shape your days: how you respond when plans fall apart, when someone disappoints you, or when old cravings and fears resurface and try to pull you back into what feels familiar. Integration shows itself in the way you celebrate small wins, how you forgive yourself for inevitable missteps, and how you stay loyal to your vision even when the world around you feels noisy or uncertain.

In my own life, integration is rarely perfect and never rigid. Sometimes it looks like returning to my grounding practices, rising early, journaling, or savoring a few breaths before the day gathers speed. Other days it arrives unexpectedly: in the delight of an honest conversation, the comfort of coffee and pan dulce with Carlos, the quiet pause of a cup of tea, or laughter at the end of a long day. There are days when integration means noticing the return of anxiety or self-doubt and, rather than following old scripts, greeting them with compassion, humor, or a gentle "Not today."

You can glimpse integration in the ways you speak to your-self in private, in how you set and honor boundaries, in the ways you receive love and offer it back to the world. Sometimes it's as simple as hearing the inner critic just as loudly as ever but choosing, perhaps for the first time, to trust the quieter voice of encouragement instead. It's looking up in a difficult moment and realizing you've responded differently, not because you forced it but because, through countless small acts of attention and self-love, you have quietly become someone new.

Integration is also the courage to return when you drift. It does not mean you never falter or lose your way. It means you know how to come back, again and again, without shame or judgment. Over time, these returns become shorter, softer, and more frequent, until returning to yourself feels less like an effort and more like the gentle rhythm of your own breath. This is the quiet revolution: living a life where wholeness is not a rare peak but a quiet, everyday practice.

THE SPIRAL, NOT THE LADDER: THE TRUE SHAPE OF INTEGRATION

Many people imagine integration, healing, and growth as a ladder: always upward, direct, and linear. But real transformation rarely works that way. Integration is a spiral, a looping and living journey where you return to familiar places and old patterns, each time with greater awareness, new tools, and deeper compassion.

It is not failure to revisit your challenges or to circle back to themes you thought you had resolved. In fact, this returning is often a sign of progress. Each loop of the spiral brings a little more wisdom and a little less shame, allowing you to gather what you need with every revolution.

We do not graduate from our humanity. We spiral through it, honoring every return as an opportunity for healing and integration. The myth of arrival begins to fade, replaced by the gentle rhythm of your own unfolding.

Vignette: Fatima's Circle

Fatima was a scientist, brilliant, methodical, her world built on logic and predictability. For years, she trusted the linear path: hypothesis, experiment, result. But when a wave of personal and professional upheavals swept through her life, the old frameworks stopped working. She felt lost and frustrated, unable to think her way to healing or to plot a straight path to wholeness.

In our work together, Fatima began to see her growth not as a straight line but as a circle, a spiral, an organic process of returning to familiar challenges, but now with new eyes and a softer heart. At first, the idea that progress could mean looping back was unsettling, even radical. Yet as she allowed herself to spiral, Fatima experienced a quiet relief and new freedom. She realized that integration is not about fixing everything at once or "leveling up" endlessly. It is about honoring the natural rhythm of becoming, trusting that every revisit, every return, is another layer of healing, another step toward wholeness.

For a scientist, this was a shift from control to curiosity, from certainty to trust. But for all of us, it is the gateway to authentic, sustainable transformation.

INTEGRATION AS A DAILY RHYTHM

Integration isn't a special event or distant destination. It's a living rhythm, quietly woven through the ordinary days and simple moments. It's the art of bringing your wholeness into every space you inhabit, letting your values, your needs, your quirks, and your longings flow together rather than tucking away different pieces for different rooms or different roles.

Jacob, a doctoral student, once lived a life of compartments: therapy clients here, academic work there, self-care only if there was time. His days felt fragmented, as if he were living several separate lives at once. But as Jacob leaned into the practice of integration, he began to experiment with a new kind of daily rhythm, one that gently wove together all his parts. He practiced a few mindful breaths before seeing clients, journaled short reflections after teaching, and slowly began to treat creative play and rest as essential, not optional. They became as much a part of his work as the checklists and deadlines ever were.

Integration didn't end with his own well-being. Jacob began to bring this perspective into his work with others, sharing mindfulness tools, modeling vulnerability, and inviting clients to discover their own rhythms, not just their diagnoses. The ripple was immediate. His clients felt more seen and supported, and Jacob found his days softer, more sustainable, more alive. Integration let him show up as both helper and human, teacher and learner, all at once. Jacob's integration deepened when he shared it with others, revealing that our personal alignment thrives best when mirrored and supported by community.

True integration is visible in the quiet choices: how you structure your day, how you bring your values into your work, your relationships, your moments of rest. It is the freedom to move through life as a whole person, not a collection of boxes to be checked or masks to be worn.

Prompt

You might pause and ask, How could you bring more integration into your daily routines? Where could your values, your practices, and your well-being flow together rather than living in separate boxes? Even the smallest experiment, perhaps a pause, a breath, a blending of roles, can begin to shift the whole day.

Micropractice: Blending the Day

Before you move on, take a quiet moment.Look at your day, either what's just happened or what's ahead.Notice one place where you tend to divide yourself, perhaps work and home, giving and receiving, rest and productivity.

Ask yourself: What's one small way I could let these parts meet, even for a moment? Maybe it's a breath of mindfulness before opening your laptop. Maybe it's bringing a favorite song or ritual into your work space. Maybe it's letting a pause between tasks become a chance to check in with your body or spirit.

Try it once. Notice how it feels.Integration begins with the smallest acts, a willingness to experiment, to weave, to blur the old boundaries just a bit.

INTEGRATION AND ADVANCED NEUROSCIENCE

Modern neuroscience offers us powerful metaphors and real hope for what integration truly means. Daniel Siegel's interpersonal neurobiology describes integration as the healthy linkage of distinct brain regions: emotion with reason, past with present, self with other. When these inner landscapes are able to communicate and connect, you find yourself with greater flexibility, more creativity, less reactivity, and a deepening well of empathy. You become more able to respond rather than react to life's challenges, adapting rather than breaking down.

By contrast, trauma and old survival patterns are really the story of disconnection. Circuits fragment; the body splits from feeling, or the mind races without an anchor. In that fragmented state, it's hard to respond authentically or to feel at home within yourself.

But here's the hope: Every time you consciously bring together your feelings, your values, your intentions, and your actions, whether through journaling, ritual, mindful movement, or honest conversation, you are gently re-networking your nervous system. You create new pathways, inviting your brain and body to experience wholeness that may once have felt impossible. Even the simplest practices, perhaps a few mindful breaths, five minutes of writing, a quiet ritual of gratitude, can dramatically shift your sense of coherence, agency, and possibility.

Integration is not only a psychological or spiritual journey. It is a biological revolution, a gentle rewiring for greater presence, compassion, and creativity. Each act of integration is a signal to your nervous system that it's safe to come home. Just as the brain finds wholeness through connection, so does our sense of identity when we embrace our complex, layered selves.

Practice: *Brain Integration Ritual*

Choose an event or emotion from your day. Write about it from three perspectives:

How does it feel in your body?

What thoughts or beliefs does it bring up?

What memory, story, or image does it connect to?

Pause. Notice how seeing all sides gently gathers the fragments and weaves them into something whole. How does this shift your understanding or your sense of self?

Integration Across Borders: Identity, Home, and Belonging

María Elena was an immigrant twice over, first leaving México for the United States and now navigating a climate where her right to belong was often questioned. For María Elena, integration became much more than personal growth; it was about survival, dignity, and reclaiming her place in the world. She held fiercely to her roots--her language, food, music, and stories--while learning new ways to move and thrive in a culture that didn't always welcome her presence or her voice.

Integration for María Elena was the art of building a home within herself, a safe, sacred space she could return to even when the world outside was uncertain or unkind. It meant honoring the wisdom of her ancestors, seeking out and building community, and embracing her resilience as a daily act of gentle resistance. She discovered that wholeness was not about choosing one part of herself over another but about weaving every thread, past and present, here and there, into the living tapestry of her life.

María Elena's story reminds us that integration is both a personal and a political act, a courageous reclaiming of wholeness and belonging in a world often marked by fragmentation and exclusion.

Prompt

Where in your story do you feel like an outsider or as if you straddle more than one world?

How might integration help you claim all of who you are and feel at home wherever you are?

INTEGRATION AND EMBODIMENT: MAKING WHOLENESS REAL

Integration is not just a shift in mindset or a change in perspective, it's something you come to embody. It lives in your muscles, your breath, your posture, and the small rituals that carry you through your day. True integration happens in the nervous system: the deep sense that you are safe enough to show up fully, the feeling that your gestures and habits are quietly aligned with your deepest intentions.

Sometimes you may notice your body relax in places that once brought anxiety. Other times you'll find that choices that once felt forced—nourishing meals, a walk outside, the gentle setting of a boundary—now arise naturally, as if your whole self is moving in concert.

Even your breath can become a living reminder that you are whole, present, and resilient. Embodiment is how integration becomes real, not a lofty idea but a felt sense of coherence and aliveness that you carry into each interaction and decision.

Embodiment Practice

Choose a daily ritual, such as stretching, walking, mindful breathing, dancing, or simply savoring a meal, that helps you feel your wholeness in your body. As you practice, notice how integration is not just a mental exercise but a physical experience. Let your body teach you what it means to be unified, present, and alive.

Somatic Integration Practice

Sit quietly and scan your body from head to toe. Notice areas of ease, tension, flow, or discomfort. Ask "Where do I feel most integrated? Where do I feel scattered or fragmented?"

Place a hand on your heart, your belly, or anywhere that needs care. Breathe deeply into that space, and imagine the energy of integration, calm, strong, unified, flowing through you.

Let each breath anchor you in your wholeness. Return to this practice whenever life feels fragmented or you want to come home to yourself.

Integration is a living practice. The more you allow it to take root in your body, the more natural, grounded, and sustainable your transformation becomes.

MULTICULTURAL WISDOM AND COLLECTIVE INTEGRATION

Integration is never just a private affair. All around the world, across centuries, cultures have understood what modern life so often forgets: Wholeness is forged in community. Through rites of passage, storytelling, song, shared meals, grieving and celebration, protest and movement building, humanity has always reached for healing together. These are not just ceremonies for ceremony's sake; they are acts of survival, resilience, and radical solidarity.

Especially now, when diversity, equity, and inclusion are under open attack and conversations about race, history, and justice are silenced or erased, collective integration becomes a revolutionary act. To gather in shared tradition, to mourn and celebrate together, to reclaim our stories and our places at the table, is to resist fragmentation and refuse to let fear or oppression have the final word.

Vignette: The Ubuntu CircleIn parts of Africa, the concept of ubuntu, "I am because we are," stands at the heart of integration. After periods of conflict or trauma, communities gather in a circle: elders, survivors, the young, the grieving, the hopeful. Together, they share truth, sorrow, forgiveness. Not to assign blame but to reclaim belonging and wholeness. Here, healing is not complete until it touches everyone. The mending of the social fabric, the restoration of dignity, the willingness to be accountable and repair together, this is the wisdom the world needs most right now.

During my own time in México, I learned firsthand the power of collective ritual: the sharing of food, the beauty of Día de muertos, the honoring of saints, the gathering in plazas or on the street. These are not simply traditions; they are vital acts of communal wholeness and resistance to erasure. They remind us, over and over, that no one returns to wholeness alone. Identity, hope, and healing are always woven with others.

In a society that often prizes individualism, and in a time when difference is under threat, reclaiming multicultural integration is more urgent than ever. It is an act of remembering what connects us all, of honoring the ancestors and elders whose wisdom endures in stories, recipes, songs, and resistance. If you feel fragmented, lost, or alone, seek even the smallest ways to connect: join a local gathering, share a meal, learn your neighbor's story, reach out to an old friend.

Every act of connection strengthens the larger tapestry. Your healing is never yours alone; your wholeness ripples outward in ways you may never fully see.

Prompt

Are there cultural traditions or ancestral practices in your background that nourish integration, individually or collectively?

How might you reawaken, honor, or adapt them to your own journey?

Reflection

What might integration look like for your family, your neighborhood, or your workplace?

How could your healing ripple outward?

How might you participate in the collective healing of your community, especially in times when inclusion and justice are at risk?

INTEGRATION AND NATURE

Nature, in her endless cycles, is one of our most patient and profound teachers of integration. In the forest, death becomes life as fallen leaves enrich the soil, feeding the next generation of green. The river welcomes every new current and bit of sediment, letting its path be shaped by every encounter, every obstacle. The desert holds both emptiness and abundance, beauty in starkness, resilience in scarcity. Nothing is wasted. Nothing is left out. Every part is transformed and given a place in the whole.

When integration feels stuck or impossible, when you feel scattered, or the world feels fragmented, nature can gently restore your sense of belonging and hope. A walk in a garden, the slow tending of a houseplant, a familiar path beneath your feet, or simply resting beneath a tree can remind you: Wholeness isn't about perfection. It's about honoring every season, every loss, every change. Even the storms and decay are needed for new growth. Nature is never in a rush. She does not force her parts into rigid boxes. Instead, she trusts the slow unfolding, the dance of balance over time.

Practice

Spend some time, an hour if you can, or just a few breaths, in a natural place: your backyard, a park, a garden, or even a patch of sunlight by your window. Let your attention rest on how life and decay, stillness and change, coexist and interact.

You might ask, What does this place have to teach me about being whole? Notice what you feel in your body as you slow down, and let nature's quiet, living integration speak to your own journey.

INTEGRATION AND CREATIVITY: REWEAVING THE STORY

Creative expression is one of the oldest and most powerful ways to accelerate integration. When you write, draw, sing, move, or build, you invite new pathways to form, connecting parts of your brain, your story, and your spirit that may not have touched before. Through creativity, you gently reweave the threads of memory, hope, pain, and possibility into something whole.

Vignette: Nora's CanvasNora, a trauma survivor, found that painting opened new doors where words alone had stalled. She began to integrate language and image, sometimes painting what she could not yet speak. With every brush-stroke, memories and dreams wove together, forming a new sense of self. Each finished piece became a milestone and a quiet message: I am more than my wounds.

Advanced Practice

Try creating a life map, using drawings, magazine images, or simple symbols for the different chapters of your journey. Let your hands move without judgment. As you work, notice the threads that connect even the most unrelated experiences. What new insights or patterns begin to emerge?

RETURNING, RECALIBRATING, AND REPAIRING

Integration is not a straight road; it means accepting that you will drift, lose balance, or get distracted, again and again. The heart of wholeness is in the returning: Each gentle recalibration, each willingness to come back, is itself an act of healing.

Troubleshooting

If you catch yourself slipping into old patterns such as perfectionism,

avoidance, self-doubt, pause. Take three slow, nourishing breaths.

Name what's happening, without judgment or blame. Gently ask yourself,

What do I need right now? Then offer yourself one small act of care:

a glass of water, a short walk, a word of compassion or encouragement.

Integration is about grace, not about force. Each gentle return is a stitch in the living tapestry of your new life. Remember, integration doesn't mean perfection or permanent stability. It means trusting your capacity to return home again and again, even when the path feels uncertain.

DEEPER TROUBLESHOOTING: WHEN INTEGRATION FEELS ELUSIVE

Setbacks and seasons of feeling fragmented are not failures; they are natural, even after years of growth. Sometimes wholeness seems to slip away. In those times, gentle, advanced practices can help you find your way back, no matter how far you've wandered.

You might set aside a few moments each week for an integration check-in. Pause and ask yourself: Where do I feel whole? Where do I feel scattered? What part of me needs attention or gentleness right now? These small questions can begin to illuminate the places that are ready for more care.

At the end of a season, whether spring or autumn or simply a chapter in your life, you could review your journals or memories, celebrating wins and noticing where your spiral deepened. Mark the milestones, honor the returns, and let yourself witness your own progress.

And when your mind fragments, you can return to your senses—smell, touch, taste—as anchors to the present. Sometimes it's the warmth of a cup, the scent of rain, the softness of a blanket, or the taste of something nourishing that brings you home to your body and your now.

Vignette: Embodied Grounding

Nico, who lives with anxiety, carries a smooth stone in his pocket. Each time stress rises, he squeezes the stone and quietly names something he's grateful for. This tiny act becomes a lifeline, a somatic reminder that no matter the chaos outside or inside, integration is always available. The body, the senses, gratitude, these become steady hands, guiding him back to center.

INTEGRATION ACROSS DIFFERENCE: CULTURE, COMMUNITY, AND JUSTICE

True integration honors both your singularity and your belonging. For some, it means reconciling identities, maybe race, ethnicity, gender, sexuality, spirituality, that the world has insisted cannot coexist. For others, it means learning to hold personal truth and community responsibility side by side. Integration asks you to become whole not by erasing your differences but by weaving them together into something uniquely, powerfully yours.

Vignette: Khalil's Bridge

Khalil grew up between worlds: his family's traditions on one side, the openness of the wider world on the other. For him, integration wasn't about choosing one or the other but about drawing nourishment from both. He cooked his grandmother's recipes while building his chosen family and spoke his mother tongue and his own truth, even when it was difficult. Over time, his life became a bridge, not a battleground but a quiet invitation to others: You can belong to yourself and your people, all at once.

Integration is also a matter of resilience, especially in uncertain times. It is not about bouncing back to what was but bouncing forward, letting every challenge, every loss, every pivot become part of your wholeness.

Vignette: Surviving the Storm

When Lucía lost her job during the pandemic, her sense of self unraveled. Old anxieties and scarcity stories surged up. Integration for Lucía meant letting herself grieve, honoring her panic, and still reaching for daily practices: gratitude lists, walks, virtual circles of support. What emerged was not her old self but a deeper, more adaptive identity. Integration was not a return but the unfolding of who she was becoming.

Reflection:As you consider your own journey: your differences, your challenges, your unique tapestry of belonging, notice what threads you are weaving right now.

Where do you find yourself building bridges between parts of your identity, your community, or your story?

How might you honor the wholeness that is quietly emerging, even if it does not look as you once imagined?

You might close your eyes, place a hand on your heart, and acknowledge the resilience you have already shown. Each step, each return, each act of self-acceptance is shaping a new way of being, one that holds room for all of you and for all who walk beside you.

And so, in honor of everyone who has courageously built bridges, embraced their wholeness, and forged belonging on their own terms, Lucille Clifton's words offer a powerful blessing, an affirmation of resilience and self-created identity:

won't you celebrate with me

by Lucille Clifton

> won't you celebrate with me
> what i have shaped into
> a kind of life? i had no model.
> born in babylon
> both nonwhite and woman
> what did i see to be except myself?
> i made it up
> here on this bridge between
> starshine and clay,
> my one hand holding tight
> my other hand; come celebrate
> with me that everyday
> something has tried to kill me
> and has failed.

Let these lines be a touchstone, a reminder that your bridge-work, your becoming, and your courage are worth celebrating, every single day.

PRACTICES FOR INTEGRATION

Integration is cultivated by gentle repetition, honest reflection, and celebration, sometimes subtle, sometimes bold. The following practices are invitations, not prescriptions. Try what calls to you, and let the rest wait for another season.

Integration Inventory:

In your journal, reflect on the journey you've taken so far. What has shifted? What new habits, beliefs, or ways of being are taking root? Where do you still feel challenged or tender? Notice how your responses to old triggers or cycles may have changed, even if just a little. Let your writing honor both progress and imperfection.

Integration Ritual:

Mark your progress with a simple ritual. You might light a candle, write a letter to your former self, or create a collage of images that mirror your new alignment. Let ritual make the invisible visible and give shape to your transformation.

Integration Circle:

Gather with trusted friends, colleagues, or a supportive group to share your stories and listen to theirs. Witnessing and being witnessed deepens integration. This is how private work becomes communal healing and how shared humanity becomes a resource for growth.

Living Questions:

Carry a question with you into the week: How can I live my alignment today, in this moment, in this challenge? Let this question guide your daily choices and gentle course corrections. Sometimes, living the question is the most integrated act you can offer.

Creative Practice:

Let creativity weave you back together. Draw, paint, or make music that reflects your journey. Sometimes the hand or the voice can reach places that words alone cannot.

INTEGRATION AND THE BODY: SOMATIC ANCHORING (ADVANCED)

True integration lives in the body. When you move, breathe, and rest with intention, you give all parts of yourself a chance to return home. Try this practice when you feel scattered or whenever you want to anchor your wholeness a little more deeply:

Advanced Somatic Integration Practice

Lie on the floor or sit comfortably. With each inhale, imagine gathering all the parts of yourself that feel scattered or forgotten. With each exhale, release tension and quietly call those parts home. Gently move, stretch, sway, shake, letting your body lead the rhythm of integration.

Afterward, journal about any sensations, images, or feelings that arose. Let the practice be slow, spiral, and kind.

Prompt

How does your body let you know when you are aligned or out of sync?

What somatic cues signal wholeness for you?

Notice what you discover, not just in your thoughts but in your breath, your heartbeat, your posture, your way of being present.

INTEGRATION AS ONGOING EVOLUTION

Integration is never truly finished; it is always unfolding, always evolving. Each day offers a fresh invitation to live your alignment and to gather the lessons that life presents, even when those lessons arrive disguised as setbacks. Each new challenge, dream, or stage of life invites another round of reflection, embodiment, and gentle return to center.

Integration also asks you to honor your past selves: every version of you who tried, failed, succeeded, loved, lost, and kept going. Each one is a necessary thread woven into the fabric of your wholeness.

Vignette: The Wise Elder Within

At seventy, Santiago reflected quietly on how often he had reinvented himself as teacher, artist, caretaker, grandfather. "Each chapter felt like starting over," he said, "But really, I was always adding to the whole." For Santiago, integration meant listening with humility and gratitude to all the voices of his life, letting each chapter guide him gently forward. He knew that every return was not a detour but a deepening of his wholeness.

ADVANCED INTEGRATION: BECOMING THE TEACHER

Integration is never only about you, it's about what you choose to do with who you have become. As you spiral into deeper wholeness, you may find within yourself a new desire emerging: the wish to share, teach, model, or support others on their paths. This does not require formal expertise or title; it simply asks for your willingness to be visible in your growth, embodying your wisdom as an offering and a gift.

Here are some gentle pathways toward becoming the teacher:

Modeling wholeness

Live your alignment openly, demonstrating to others how to return to center, forgive yourself, and honor your needs.

Storytelling as teaching

Share your story honestly, celebrating your victories and naming your setbacks, inviting others to trust that their journeys matter too.

Creating community

Form or join a group, circle, or virtual gathering space to share stories, reflect, and grow together, knowing that collective healing is deeply powerful.

Mentorship and sponsorship

Offer support to those just beginning their journeys; sometimes one encouraging gesture can gently change the course of a life.

Advocacy and allyship

Use your voice to help create a world that is more just, more inclusive, and more whole for everyone.

Prompt

What might it look like for you to become the teacher in your own gentle way, within your own circles?

Where could your journey of integration inspire or quietly support others, even if you never speak a word?

INTEGRATION IN TIMES OF LOSS, GRIEF, AND CHANGE

Integration becomes especially tender and powerful in times of transition. Loss, illness, relocation, endings of relationships, or any deep shift can leave you feeling scattered, as though parts of yourself have drifted apart. During these times, the quiet, courageous work of integration means gathering what's true, honoring your grief, and gently rebuilding a sense of meaning, connection, and wholeness.

If you find yourself in a time of grief or upheaval, your journal can become a safe harbor. Write softly about what you miss, about what has shifted, and about what remains true at your core. Reach toward practices, rituals, or people who remind you, even subtly, that wholeness is still possible, even amid uncertainty.

Prompt

Who or what helps you remember your wholeness when life feels fragmented?

Are there rituals or gentle reminders you can create to honor your journey and reconnect with your sense of self?

INTEGRATION AND LEGACY: WHOLENESS AS YOUR GIFT TO THE WORLD

Integration is never only for you. It ripples outward, quietly shaping the world that will come after. The more whole you become, the more your presence, wisdom, and compassion offer permission for others to trust their own journeys. Your healing, in ways both seen and unseen, becomes part of a greater tapestry.

Vignette: The Grandmother's Quilt

In many cultures, elders make quilts from scraps of fabric, with each square holding a memory, a season, a prayer. The finished quilt, rich in color and variety, is beautiful precisely because it gathers so many diverse threads. Your integrated life is much like this quilt: a patchwork of struggle and celebration, sorrow and joy, experience and insight, that warms everyone it touches.

Take a gentle moment to honor this quiet truth: Your integration is a living legacy, a gift offered not just to yourself but to every life you touch.

CELEBRATION AND INTEGRATION: MARKING THE JOURNEY

Celebration is the gentle act that cements your integration. We too often rush past our own growth, hungry for the next goal, never fully honoring the distance we've traveled. Take intentional moments, monthly, quarterly, or whenever your heart calls you, to reflect on your journals, revisit your journey, and honor your milestones, large and small.

Ritual

Consider hosting an integration dinner, a gathering of friends or loved ones, sharing stories, blessings, and insights for the road ahead. Alternatively, write a letter to your future self, lovingly promising to remember what matters most and offering encouragement to return, again and again, to your wholeness.

Reflection Prompts for Deepening Integration

Use these prompts gently and regularly to deepen your awareness and anchor your integration:

What parts of myself have I welcomed home since beginning this journey?

Where do I still notice tension or disconnection, and what might these places need?

Who has witnessed my process, and how can I express my gratitude?

How will I remind myself, during the next storm, that integration is always possible?

When was the last time I felt utterly whole?

What are three resources--people, places, practices--that help me return to center?

What treasures have I discovered in my cracks or wounds?

Closing Ritual: The Quilt of Wholeness

To close your reflection, take a quiet moment, perhaps place your hands gently over your heart, and breathe.

Imagine your life as a quilt, vibrant with colors, textures, memories, and dreams. Each square represents part of your journey: joy, sorrow, transitions, and growth.

Softly bring to mind one memory or experience from your past that feels especially alive right now. Then, imagine another square representing your present, the person you are becoming at this very moment. Feel how beautifully both squares belong together, side by side, gently stitched in place by your life's experience.

With your next breath, silently affirm:

Every part of my journey matters.

Every piece is welcome here.

My wholeness is a gift, both to myself and to the world.

When you're ready, gently release your hands. Carry this quiet awareness forward, knowing integration is a living practice, always available, always deepening, always yours.

THE ENDLESS INVITATION: INTEGRATION AS LIFELONG PROCESS

Integration is the work of a lifetime, an ongoing invitation to return, deepen, and evolve. The spiral will always turn again, bringing familiar lessons with fresh wisdom, challenges met with newfound grace. Each time you gather your fragments and make space for your whole self, you quietly bring the world a bit closer to its own wholeness too.

Let your integration be generous, radiating outward through your words, your presence, your quiet moments of courage. Remember that you are never truly starting over. You are simply walking another round of the spiral, each step gently guiding you home.

Integration is a living, evolving practice. As you continue on this path, your story will unfold in ways you could never predict. The next and final chapter of this journey will bring together all these threads, not just as teachings but as lived, felt experience. I'll share reflections on revising this work, the subtle ways my own journey has transformed, and insights that can only come from looking back with as much compassion as we look forward.

In this closing chapter, we will explore how alignment is never finished, how our stories spiral, deepen, and enrich over time and how together we're called to step forward, again and again, into the quiet, profound magic of what is possible right here, right now. Carry this gentle awareness forward, trusting that the threads you've gathered here will help you weave your journey into an ever-deepening, integrated wholeness.

10. RETURNING HOME: THE SPIRAL OF AUTHENTIC TRANSFORMATION

> True strength is forged in the darkest moments; it is there that you discover your capacity to endure and be reborn.

> — FRIDA KAHLO

As I WRITE these final pages, the sun gently sets over Querétaro, México, a city that has gracefully evolved into my home. The journey to this place, and more importantly, the journey within, continues to surprise and guide me. Revising this book has been more than mere reflection; it has become a living practice of integration, a profound emergence into new depths of authenticity.

The person who began this edition no longer exists. My life's landscape continually transforms, and the deeper I listen, the clearer I understand: True transformation is rarely about achieving something "out there." Instead, it is a quiet, powerful returning, again and again, to the essential truth of who I am.

If there is one resounding lesson, it's that growth never truly ends. Our true path is a spiral, not a straight line. As we move forward, we inevitably circle back, each turn bringing a bit more wisdom, a bit less fear, and a deeper readiness to welcome ourselves home. Every reading, every writing, every new season enriches the spiral. What once felt foreign now feels warmly familiar; what once appeared as a distant goal effortlessly becomes a gentle way of being.

And I must be honest: revising *A Life Aligned* has led me into some dark, uncomfortable places. It has been laborious in every sense, requiring me to confront my deepest fears, anxieties, and uncertainties. At times it felt like being tossed into shadowy depths, stripped of familiar distractions, compelled to sit with unsettling truths about who I have been and who I am becoming. In these moments, the powerful words of Frida Kahlo return: "La verdadera fuerza se forja en los momentos más oscuros; es justo ahí donde descubres tu capacidad para aguantar y volver a nacer." ("True strength is forged in the darkest moments; it is there that you discover your capacity to endure and be reborn.")

Earlier today, when the power went out and my familiar world slipped into silence, I was left only with my thoughts and darkness. It felt as though life itself was inviting—indeed, gently insisting—that I inhabit what I once called the neutral zone. But this place has revealed itself to be far more profound. It is not merely transitional; it is a sacred threshold between identities. It feels disorienting not because I am lost but because I am unwilling to continue as I once was, yet uncertain about who I am becoming. In this sacred pause, what I thought I knew begins to gently dissolve, allowing what I have always known at my core to surface. My role is not to rush through this delicate transition but to inhabit it consciously, gently, and reverently. Here, in this liminal heart of transformation, navigation is unnecessary. Here, we are simply and profoundly remade.

If you find yourself circling back, caught in the spiral or facing the quiet intensity of your own becoming, remember this: You are not alone. True transformation is forged here, not in the comfortable glow of easy days but in your honest, patient willingness to sit deeply with yourself, even when it feels difficult. Returning home, again and again, is the true path. And with every gentle return, you are reborn anew.

A NEW SEASON OF IMPACT AND SERVICE

Recently, my path has gently opened into new dimensions, inviting me beyond the familiar role of teacher and into the expansive territory of leader, architect, and steward. As I step deeper into administrative roles, shaping programs, mentoring faculty, and nurturing the next generation of healers and changemakers, I find myself simultaneously humbled and awakened by the magnitude of this opportunity and responsibility. No longer simply a classroom guide, I am now called to architect a culture of growth, possibility, and authentic alignment within the institutions I serve.

This work is exhilarating and profoundly humbling. It is an honor to help students not only master their disciplines but also more fully become themselves, to witness their vulnerabilities and victories as they journey through doctoral paths, professional growth, and the unpredictable demands of a rapidly shifting world. My role now feels less about dispensing knowledge and more about quietly holding sacred space: a space welcoming new ideas, messy humanity, courage, and grace. The most meaningful transformations are rarely grand or immediate; they are subtle, quiet shifts in perception, the gentle yet profound moment when someone finds their voice and dares to speak their truth aloud.

Every day, I am reminded that ripples of alignment and integrity stretch far beyond what we can measure. As a mentor, leader, and colleague, I am called to embody authenticity, resilience, and kindness, not only for myself but also for everyone whose life touches mine. The energy and presence I carry into each interaction truly matter; these unseen forces shape the culture, the climate, and the sense of possibility available to others.

Yet beyond any title or formal role, what has shifted most profoundly within me is a deeper sense of accountability for the presence and energy I offer. My task has become more than teaching or guiding: it is about embodying curiosity, flexibility, and the humility inherent in being a perpetual learner. With every interaction, with students, colleagues, friends, even strangers, I pause to silently reflect: Am I fully present? Am I living in alignment with my deepest values? Am I extending an authentic invitation for growth, not only to others but gently back to myself?

This new season is not about arrival or finality but about returning, again and again, to service as a living practice, to leadership as deep listening, and to the courageous, ongoing work of alignment in all that I am, in all that I do.

SETTLING DEEPER INTO MÉXICO, AND INTO MYSELF

My life in México continues to gently surprise me with its richness, its contrasts, and its daily invitations, encouraging me to slow down, to look a bit closer, and to truly pay attention. With each passing season, I understand more deeply that home isn't simply a fixed place or a familiar set of comforts. Rather, home is a layered, evolving experience, an ongoing invitation to open once again to what is new and unfamiliar around me and, equally, to recognize what has always been quietly familiar within myself.

At first, my attention naturally rested upon surface details: the lyrical rhythm of a new language, the gentle echo of evening church bells, the curious intricacies of navigating government offices, and those quiet, satisfying triumphs, understanding a joke shared casually by a neighbor or arranging a simple repair on my own. These moments, initially markers of survival and proof that I was indeed finding my way, were merely the doorway to something deeper.

Slowly, patiently, something richer has unfolded. I've learned to savor the leisurely lunches stretching into the warmth of the afternoon sun, to delight in sudden bursts of music drifting from an open window, to allow friendships to gently reshape me, friendships that refuse to follow the familiar scripts of my old life. As a card-carrying introvert, these are risks I once hesitated to take. But now I find myself accepting invitations I might previously have declined, not because I am fluent or flawless but because I am willing. Willing to risk being awkward, willing to be truly seen, and willing to allow others to know me as I authentically am.

My sense of belonging is no longer measured by how effortlessly I fit in but rather by how courageously I show up as myself. Here in México, I have been welcomed into rituals and celebrations rich with generations of meaning, gatherings deeply rooted in land, ancestry, and community. I have begun to understand how the land, the people, and their shared history subtly shape every story, including my own. The invitation is not merely to adapt but to willingly allow myself to be gently transformed.

Certainly, there are days when Santa Fe softly calls to me, moments when I feel a familiar longing for old comforts. Yet more and more, I realize I am not simply living in México; México is quietly and gently living within me. I find myself softer around the edges, more forgiving of myself and of others, and more open to the quiet unfolding of each new day. The process of settling into this new life has become inseparable from the profound process of settling more deeply into myself, marked by a deeper curiosity, a genuine humility, and a sense of gratitude I never imagined possible.

Not long ago, during a Christmas gathering hosted by Carlos, his husband Victor, and their families, I sat at a table overflowing with delicious dishes and rich with laughter––a deeper, warmer laughter than I had felt in years. Stories unfolded naturally, of loved ones now passed, of cherished family traditions, of hopeful dreams for the year ahead. Listening, I caught only fragments of Spanish but clearly felt the warmth and welcome in every gesture, every gentle teasing laugh, every filled plate quietly offered without question.

What struck me most profoundly was this simple yet extraordinary truth: Although I was not born here, though I carry an accent that will forever gently reveal my roots, I was included as family. No one asked me to be anyone other than who I am. And there, at Carlos and Victor's table, I understood in my bones that true belonging is not about where we begin but about where we are openly invited, accepted exactly as we are, and gently encouraged to be changed by love.

NAVIGATING FAMILY AND POLITICAL DIFFERENCES

If settling into México has quietly taught me what home truly means, then navigating family and political differences has equally taught me the profound meaning of boundaries, and of love.

Like so many others, my family is a tapestry woven from passionate opinions, strong personalities and, perhaps more prominently now than ever before, deeply divergent political views. Living abroad in México sometimes magnifies this distance. From here, I watch my loved ones in the United States wrestle with complex questions of justice and inclusion, of fear and hope. At times, I see choices and beliefs that appear to prioritize individual interests over collective well-being or overlook very real impacts on the lives of others. There are moments when conversations turn tense, words inadvertently sting, or when silence becomes the quiet refuge to maintain peace.

Yet, what I am slowly learning, sometimes with pain, sometimes with grace, is that authentic transformation does not mean turning away from those who see the world differently. Nor does it require me to abandon my own truths simply for the sake of harmony. Instead, it involves a delicate, ongoing discernment: When do I gently engage, and when do I lovingly step back? How do I listen deeply, compassionately, even when I profoundly disagree? When do I hold firmly to my values, and when do I choose connection over the need to be right?

There are times I must allow myself to mourn what feels lost, perhaps a closeness that can't easily be reclaimed, or the quiet dream of perfect understanding. Yet, small bridges sometimes appear in the gentle flow of life: a shared memory, a spontaneous laugh, or a quiet, sincere "love you" that rises gently above differences. There is profound strength in loving someone enough to accept them exactly as they are, without betraying my own heart or conscience. My practice now is to keep my door softly open, even as I hold clear and loving boundaries. To remember gently that, beneath all the noise, most of us quietly seek the same simple, profound things: safety, belonging, a meaningful life, and the comfort of being truly seen.

Living at this crossroads of cultures and beliefs, I am reminded daily that real transformation quietly emerges from one honest conversation at a time, especially those conversations that feel difficult. True transformation is rarely about winning arguments or erasing differences. Instead, it is about standing gently yet firmly in my own truth while generously extending grace. Sometimes the most courageous act possible is simply to hold both clarity and kindness, conviction and connection, quietly honoring each.

Prompt

Where in your life are you quietly being called to stand firmly in your truth while also extending gentle grace to someone who sees the world through a different lens?

AUTHENTIC TRANSFORMATION: MY ONGOING PRACTICE

Transformation is not a trophy to be won, nor a static state to be preserved. It is an ongoing, living practice, a dance that asks for both courage and humility, for joy and grief, for surrender and creative will. Every day, I am reminded that authentic transformation is as much about the willingness to revisit old patterns as it is about celebrating new growth.

There are days when I feel accomplished, deeply connected, and alive with possibility. And there are days when loneliness returns or doubt creeps in, when the grief of the past quietly surfaces, or the magnitude of the world's suffering feels heavy on my heart. What has changed is not that these moments have vanished but that my relationship to them has softened.

I root myself in daily rituals: journaling in the quiet before sunrise, lighting a candle to anchor my intention, letting gratitude shape my evening reflections. I lean into the wisdom of mentors, the ancient traditions that have outlasted generations, and the everyday teachings offered by those around me––students, friends, strangers in the street. Above all, I allow myself to be a student of life, always learning, always adjusting, always becoming.

Sometimes, the return to alignment finds me in the most unexpected moments. Lately, it's happened through long, enlightening conversations with my friend Uriel, whose art will soon bring this book's spirit to life. These hours together are more than just creative planning, they're a practice of mutual seeing, a gentle opening into new perspectives. In Uriel's way of looking at the world, I find aspects of myself reflected back, sometimes illuminated for the first time. And I know our connection is mutual: as we explore, wonder, and question together, each of us becomes more visible to ourselves and to each other. Through Uriel's perceptions as an artist, I am reminded that this kind of relational, creative dialogue is not a distraction from the "real work" of my days but is instead what makes all the rest possible. It is a vital way home to myself.

When I stumble (as I inevitably do), I return to my tools: a conscious breath, a gentle pause, the steady grounding of my body, the quiet reminder that all feelings are welcome and every story belongs. When I drift from alignment, I now know how to return, not with shame or urgency but with a kind of gentle curiosity. I act as if I am worthy of my own care until that feeling becomes real.

Above all, I remain open to surprise. Life in México and in the quiet, ongoing connections I hold with family, across distance, difference, and time, reminds me that I am always standing at a threshold. Each day brings an invitation to leave behind familiar certainties and step forward into what is true now, even as the path ahead remains mysterious. In my work and my becoming, I do not rush the process. I choose instead to stand here on purpose, welcoming the unexpected moments of magic and grace that arise when I am willing to be surprised: by others, by myself, and by life itself.

Vignette: The Spiral in Practice

A student recently confided, "Every time I think I've arrived, life reminds me I'm still spiraling, but I trust the process more each time." This, for me, is the quiet heart of authentic transformation. You never truly "arrive"; you become more willing to return. And each return brings new depth, new meaning, and a little more grace.

THE LONGING FOR HOME: A UNIVERSAL SPIRAL

If there is one longing that runs through every story I have witnessed or lived, it is the longing to belong, not just in a place or a relationship but to ourselves, to one another, and to something greater than our own story. At its heart, the spiral of transformation is the spiral of returning home. Over the years, I have come to see that home is not a fixed address or a single relationship but a living, evolving field, a place we both carry inside us and create anew with each conscious choice.

So many of us spend years, even lifetimes, searching for home outside ourselves: in accomplishments, in the approval of others, in the hope that a perfect set of circumstances will finally bring us peace. We chase the feeling that once we have enough, do enough, or become enough, then we'll finally belong. Yet, the spiral of authentic transformation offers a gentler, wiser truth: Belonging does not arise when the world finally fits our expectations but when we learn to honor, accept, and trust our own presence, imperfect, evolving, and real.

The journey home is not a single leap, but a series of small, daily returns. Sometimes it looks like pausing to notice a breath before responding, recognizing the voice of your inner critic and choosing not to follow it or catching yourself savoring a moment, a song on the radio, a meal, a walk, or a burst of laughter with a friend instead of racing toward the next thing. These are not just moments of self-care; they are seeds of homecoming, reminders that belonging is something you can practice and embody, right now, wherever you find yourself on the spiral.

Home is never only about geography, heritage, or even family, though all those things matter. Home is a felt sense of welcome inside your own life, a willingness to return, again and again, to your true center no matter how far you've wandered. As life unfolds and circumstances change, as you grieve, as you celebrate, as you grow, let your definition of home evolve with you. Let it be a space big enough to hold your joy, your doubt, your heritage, your hopes, and your longing for connection.

As you complete this book, I invite you to honor the subtle ways you have already begun to come home. Notice where you pause, where you soften, where you choose presence over perfection. Let these be both compass and celebration: proof that home is not something you find once and for all but something you spiral toward, create, and return to for the rest of your life.

THE COURAGE TO CLAIM YOUR STORY

Returning home also means reclaiming your story, not just the curated highlights but the raw mess, the doubts, the resilience, and those small flickers of hope that refuse to be extinguished. Our stories, in all their tangled complexity, are the gold of the spiral. The very parts you once wished to hide, the moments of failure, shame, uncertainty, or ordinary struggle, are now what make your journey powerful, relatable, and profoundly inspiring. In owning the full arc of your experience, rather than only the polished surface, you create true connection and meaning, not just for yourself but for others walking their own spirals home.

It is so easy to believe our story is too fractured, too mundane, or too unfinished to matter. We compare our behind the scenes to someone else's highlight reel and quietly decide to stay silent, wondering, "Who am I to share?" But it is precisely the courage to tell the truth of your journey, to speak honestly from the spiral and not just from the summit, that lights the way for others.

Vignette: Sharing the Story

A client named Jamie spent years believing her story was too fractured, too ordinary, too full of missteps to be of value. Yet, when she finally began to share her story with others, her setbacks, her stumbles, her imperfect triumphs, she discovered something unexpected. Her honesty became an open door, a quiet permission slip for others to begin telling their truths as well. Jamie's spiral, her ongoing, unfinished, real-as-breathing story, became a map for those just beginning their own.

Your story, too, can become a lantern in someone else's darkness. You do not need to wait until you are "finished," polished, or perfectly healed to begin sharing. Right now, standing at this threshold in the middle of your spiral, your lived experience is enough. Claim it, honor it, and let it shine, not only for your own sake but as a gift and a gentle guide to others who are finding their way home.

EMBRACING OUR COLLECTIVE AND ANCESTRAL WOUNDS

Homecoming is never only a personal journey. It is, always and inevitably, a collective and ancestral one as well. Each of us carries stories and wounds that did not begin with us, unhealed pain and silent burdens passed through families, communities, and cultures. These are the fractures shaped by histories of injustice, displacement, loss, and longing. The world itself is etched with these fault lines, and it is tempting to believe that healing is something we must do in isolation. But the spiral of authentic transformation is also the spiral of collective healing. Each time you claim your truth, honor your roots, and let your story be seen, you help mend a web that stretches far beyond your own life.

Pause for a moment and sense the ancestral stories that live quietly in your bones. Maybe you carry the memory of migration, the music of lost languages still humming beneath your breath, recipes and rituals handed down in kitchens, or the shadows of old losses beside the light of inherited strengths. Integration is the invitation to honor both pain and resilience. It is an act of courage to grieve what was lost, to name what could not be given, and also to celebrate what survived, sometimes against all odds. Sometimes integration asks you to offer forgiveness to those who could not meet you, and other times to send gratitude across the years to those who kept the thread alive, even when it was worn thin.

Perhaps you are the first in your family to break a silence, to imagine a different future, to reclaim your wholeness or your voice. This is sacred work, transformational not only for yourself but for the generations who will follow, and for the ancestors whose unfinished hopes are alive now in you. Each gentle step you take to heal, to forgive, to bless, to belong, is a gift that moves both backward and forward in time. Healing spirals through families, across generations, through communities, and into the world.

Remember, you do not walk this path alone. There is a vast unseen lineage behind you, each person who once longed for what you are now becoming. There is a widening circle beside you, others who are waking up, returning home, mending the same web with their own stories and longing and love. The spiral of healing weaves us all together.

Practice

Take a few quiet breaths. When you feel ready, write a letter of gratitude or forgiveness to an ancestor, known or unknown, thanking them for what they carried, for what they survived, and for the ways you are now continuing the spiral of healing.

Allow this simple act to shift your sense of belonging, in your own story and in the greater story we all share.

BELONGING IN THE WORLD: FROM THE PERSONAL TO THE PLANETARY

The spiral of authentic transformation does not end with self-acceptance; it gently expands outward into the world. Each time you return home to yourself, you find yourself more able, and more willing, to welcome others: across differences of culture, language, history, or belief. You realize that belonging is not only a right but also a living responsibility, a gift to be received and a practice to be shared.

Vignette: Bridge at the Mercado

In cities and villages around the world, moments of true connection unfold quietly, at a corner café, a leafy park, or the colorful bustle of a local mercado. These aren't grand occasions but simple, humble exchanges: a glance shared in line, a gentle smile from a stranger, a word of welcome spoken with no agenda. In such ordinary moments, bridges are built, wordless acknowledgments of our shared, fragile humanity.

What matters most is never perfection or fluency, but presence. Again and again, showing up as you are, awkward, imperfect, and open, becomes its own act of courage. For many of us, especially those who identify as introverts or feel culturally out of place, the willingness to risk being seen is no small thing. And yet, in that small risk lies the seed of transformation.

In a world marked by polarization and separation, these everyday gestures of alignment, these tiny homecomings, become acts of quiet revolution. When you walk the spiral, you become a bridge: in your family, your work, your neighborhood. You become the one who listens more deeply, forgives more quickly, stands up more bravely, and invites more generously. Your presence alone becomes a threshold where others, too, may glimpse a sense of home.

Returning Ritual

To honor this chapter and the path you've walked so far, try this ritual of return:

Find a quiet moment and light a candle, or settle by a window where you can see the sky.

Take three slow breaths, picturing the spiral path that has brought you here.

Speak aloud or write these words: "I am home in myself. I honor every step, every lesson, every turn of the spiral."

If you keep a journal, draw your spiral, marking the moments of pain and joy, loss and love, belonging and growth.

As you close, thank yourself for the courage to come home and imagine sending a blessing outward: to your ancestors, to your future self, and to all who are still searching for their place of belonging.

And if you feel called, consider sharing this ritual with a friend, a loved one, or your community. Remember, even the smallest act of presence, a word, a gesture, a pause, can ripple outward, lighting the path for others and weaving a wider circle of belonging in our world.

VISIONING FORWARD: THE SPIRAL NEVER ENDS

As you cross this threshold, you may notice new questions quietly arising: What now? Where does the spiral lead next? How will you carry your alignment into the wider world?

There is no single answer, no map for this next becoming. The invitation is simply to keep walking, to keep noticing, to keep inviting wonder into ordinary days. Let your values, your rituals, and your relationships be your compass. Know that when you falter or forget, the spiral will gently call you back, again and again, to the living center of your being.

Prompt

What is your next small act of homecoming?

How will you welcome yourself today, and how might you extend that welcome to someone else?

BRINGING IT ALL TOGETHER: A CALL TO ACTION

Alignment is not a one-time act; it is the way you walk, the way you listen, the way you meet each moment with curiosity, hope, and a willingness to be changed. Everything you need is already within you. What matters now is to live it, share it, and allow yourself to be transformed along the way.

So here is my invitation:

Keep showing up. Especially on the hard days, especially when you doubt, especially when the world seems upside down.

Use your journal, your rituals, and your circle of support. These are the anchors that help you return to yourself, again and again.

Share your journey. Your story, your struggles, your break-throughs are not just for you. When you share them, you become a source of hope and possibility for others, a gentle reminder that we all walk the spiral together.

Join our community. I truly would love to hear your story. I invite you to join our community at https://drmarkar curi.com where you can connect with me and with others walking their own paths of alignment. Post your reflections, your dreams, your questions, and your wisdom. Together, we create a space where magic becomes real, not through perfection but through authentic presence and shared growth.

Prompt

What is one act of courage or sharing you can commit to this month, something that honors your spiral and gently invites others onto the path with you?

LOOKING FORWARD: PARADISE (RE)DISCOVERED

As this chapter closes, another opens, and once again I find myself standing at a threshold. This revision of *A Life Aligned: The Journey to Allowing the Magic in Your Life* is profoundly different from the original, and yet it feels truer than ever to the spirit of the process. Nearly twenty years have passed since that first edition. In that time, my life has spiraled and shifted through countless changes, losses, moves, reckonings, moments of awe, and moments of darkness. I have grown in ways I could never have imagined, and so has this book.

Revising these pages has been its own crucible, a journey that at times pulled me into the shadows, stripped away distractions, and asked me to face the rawness of transition and rebirth. As Frida Kahlo so wisely reminds us, true strength is forged in the darkest moments; it is there we discover our capacity to endure, and to be reborn. That has been the heartbeat of this revision: letting go of old certainties, making peace with the spiral, and allowing a new voice and a deeper truth to come forward.

Authentic transformation, I have learned, is never a straight line nor a perfect arc. It is a living spiral. Each return, each act of courage, each willingness to sit with discomfort, each honest telling of my story, deepens my sense of home and connection. Even now, as I write these words in a city that once felt foreign and now feels like home, I know the journey is unfinished. The spiral continues to call me onward.

This is why, as this book comes to its own return, I am already deep in the next chapter of my own spiral: *Paradise (Re)Discovered: Authenticity in a New World*. There, I'll invite you even further, into questions of what it means to belong, to claim your truth in times of upheaval, and to co-create paradise right here, amid a world that rarely stands still. The work of aligning our lives is not a final destination but an ever-renewing invitation: to live, to risk, to return, and to begin again.

If you have read this far, you are part of this unfolding story. The spiral does not end here. Every ending is a new invitation. Each time you dare to come home to yourself, you set the stage for new belonging, new vision, and a new paradise, waiting to be discovered in the courage of your own becoming.

I hope you will continue this journey with me. For now, know this: The spiral continues. The invitation stands. And you, exactly as you are, in all your beautiful, imperfect humanity, are ready for what comes next.

Blessing for the Journey

May you trust your spiral.
May you know that every turn, even the dark and uncertain ones, brings you closer to your wholeness and to the home within yourself.
May you remember that you are both the traveler and the homecoming, both the seeker and the sanctuary.
May your story become a lantern for others who are finding their way, and may you be surprised, again and again, by unexpected joy and true companionship along the path.

Thank you for walking this journey with me, through all its seasons, thresholds, and returns. The spiral continues, and with each step, it opens wider.

APPENDIX -
ADVANCED PRACTICES

As your journey spirals onward , you may find yourself ready for new levels of exploration, homecoming, and growth. The following practices are invitations to deepen your act as if experience, gently stretch your comfort zone, and bring your vision even more fully to life. Each is a threshold, a doorway you can cross and return to, again and again. Choose what resonates, adapt as needed, and remember: progress is the spiral, not perfection.

The Future Self Immersion

Set aside a full afternoon or even a whole day. Imagine yourself stepping across the threshold into your next becoming. Live as if you are already your future self: the one who has embodied your intention. Dress, eat, move, work, rest, and speak as that person would. Shift your environment in small ways (music, décor, scents, even rearranging a room). If you feel brave, interact with others as your future self. At day's end, journal: What felt natural? What felt awkward? What surprised you? How did you respond to the unexpected? What new desires or insights emerged? Let this be a gentle spiral into possibility, not a performance but a homecoming to who you are becoming.

The Public Declaration

Choose an intention you've been quietly nurturing. Find a safe supportive space, perhaps it is social media, a trusted group, a friend, or a circle of kindred spirits. At the threshold of your next becoming, declare your intention aloud, as if it is already underway. For example: "I am becoming a writer." Journal about the emotions and resistance that come up before and after sharing. Notice how being witnessed changes your sense of momentum, possibility, and connection.Your declaration, imperfect and alive, is itself a powerful act of invitation and return.

The Shadow Invitation

For one week, spiral deeper by journaling about moments you hesitate, procrastinate, or act as if nothing will ever change. Gently invite your shadow, your doubt, fear, or cynicism to have a voice in your journal. Let it write you a letter. Then, as your aligned self, write back. Explore: What do you need to heal, forgive, or re-parent to act as if with more freedom and wholeness? Welcome your shadow to the threshold. Let its wisdom soften judgment and reveal new layers of self-compassion.

The Embodiment Challenge

Choose a daily ritual, movement, exercise, dance, singing, even walking. Each time you practice, consciously embody your intention. If your intention is power, stand tall and breathe deeply, even if it feels unfamiliar. After a week, reflect: Has your body's experience changed? Has your mood or confidence shifted? What feedback have you received from yourself or others?Let each movement be a spiral homecoming, a way to cross, again and again, into a new way of being.

Design Your Environment

Choose a room, a workspace, or even a digital space. Redesign it as if your intention were already a living reality. If your intention is abundance, bring beauty and order to your space. If creativity, place your tools within reach and display reminders of your craft. Notice how your environment either supports or undermines your new identity. Make changes as you feel called. Journal: What does it feel like to inhabit this new space? Your environment is a living spiral, an external invitation to deeper belonging right where you are.

Reverse Act As If--The "What If I Don't?" Exercise

For one day, pause at the threshold and intentionally notice (without judgment) what happens if you don't act as if. Observe your choices, emotions, energy, and interactions. Journal what arises. Let this be a moment of gentle curiosity, illuminating the contrast and reminding you of the power and freedom in your conscious returns.

Remember

Each of these practices is a living invitation, not a test or requirement. Let your spiral of growth be gentle, real, and alive. Celebrate every return, each one a step deeper into homecoming, presence, and the magic of your own alignment.

GLOSSARY OF KEY TERMS

Act As If : A practice, rooted in psychology and ancient wisdom, of behaving in alignment with your desired reality even before you fully believe or "are there." It's an experiment in becoming.

Alignment: Living in harmony with your deepest values, desires, and truth, where your thoughts, feelings, and actions work together rather than in opposition.

Ancestor/Ancestral Stories: The lived and inherited experiences, wounds, and wisdom passed down through generations. Ancestral stories can shape our patterns, strengths, longings, and healing work, inviting us to honor both pain and resilience as we spiral forward.

Authenticity: The courageous expression of your true self, beneath roles, expectations, or conditioning. Authenticity is not a static trait but a continual unfolding as you align more fully with who you really are, moment by moment.

Awareness: Gentle, nonjudgmental noticing of what is happening within and around you. Awareness is the foundation for all meaningful change.

Belonging: A felt sense of being seen, accepted, and valued, not for conformity but for your essence. True belonging begins within and radiates outward, creating bridges between self, others, and the world.

Blessing: A conscious expression of goodwill, hope, or gratitude, offered for oneself or others at moments of transition, return, or new beginning. A blessing marks a threshold and invites the presence of grace.

Commitment: The devotion to showing up for your intention and vision again and again, especially when it's inconvenient, uncomfortable, or uncertain.

Home: Not merely a place or relationship but a living, evolving field of belonging, a felt sense of welcome within yourself and with others. Home is continually created and rediscovered as you cross new thresholds on the spiral of your life.

Homecoming: The return to your innermost self, where you remember what matters most. Homecoming is not always tied to place, it is a felt alignment of soul, purpose, and peace. Homecoming is a continual process; each spiral return brings new depth and meaning.

Integration: The process of bringing all the parts of yourself, old and new, shadow and light, into coherence and wholeness so that your growth becomes embodied and sustainable.

Intention: A conscious choice or aim. More than a wish, intention is the energy you direct toward what you want to create or become.

Invitation: A gentle opening or call, spoken or unspoken, that welcomes you or others into new possibility, growth, or presence. The journey of alignment is filled with invitations, both subtle and bold.

Journal: Your private, trusted companion for reflection, intention, and insight, a place to witness your story as it unfolds.

Lantern: A symbol for sharing your story or presence as a source of guidance and hope for others navigating their own spiral home.

Ping and thud: A body-based way of knowing. A ping feels alive, resonant, and light; a thud feels heavy, resistant, or off. Learning to sense the difference helps guide decisions.

Presence: The act of being fully here, attentive to the moment, to yourself, and to those around you. Presence is both a practice and a gift that deepens connection and awakens possibility. Presence is the heart of belonging and the gateway to all transformation.

Shadow Work: Turning toward and gently working with the hidden, denied, or disowned parts of yourself, not to banish them but to integrate their wisdom.

Spiral: A symbol and structure of transformation that moves both inward and outward. Unlike a straight path, the spiral honors that growth often returns us to familiar themes with deeper awareness. Each turn of the spiral is a threshold, a place to pause, integrate, and begin again, always deeper than before.

Threshold: A potent moment or space between what was and what is becoming, a crossing point. Standing at the threshold means honoring both the ending and the beginning, the unknown and the possibility ahead.

Vision: Your heartfelt sense of what is possible for you and your life, an inner picture that guides, inspires, and pulls you forward.

FINAL BLESSING

May each step you take be blessed with courage, each breath a
gentle
return to your own wisdom.
May you find beauty in the unexpected, belonging wherever you
pause,
and love, always love, waiting for you, within and all around.
Your story matters.
Your journey is sacred.
May you walk in magic, and know you are never alone.

ABOUT THE AUTHOR

Mark is a psychologist, educator, and transformational guide whose work weaves together science, spirit, and soul. For more than thirty years, he has helped individuals and groups discover the freedom and magic of living a life aligned, one rooted in vision, intention, and authentic action.

He is known for his integrative approach, blending clinical expertise with a deep respect for ancient wisdom, positive psychology, the law of attraction, and embodied mind–body practices. Mark serves as a faculty member and administrator in doctoral programs, where he mentors future healers and agents of change, both in person and virtually, in clinical psychology and mind–body medicine.

Born and raised in the United States of America, Mark now calls Querétaro, México home. His personal journey, from New York to South Florida to Dallas to Santa Fe to México, from therapist to teacher to community builder, continues to spiral through his life and work, informing every page he writes. He knows firsthand the beauty and challenge of crossing borders, not only between countries as an immigrant but within the unfolding landscapes of the self.

Mark's work centers on the belief that alignment is available to everyone and that the journey is as meaningful as any destination. When he's not writing or teaching, you'll find him wandering the back streets of Querétaro, savoring good food with friends, journaling at sunrise, or quietly cheering on the dreams of others. He especially treasures spirited conversations and creative collaborations where insight, laughter, and new possibilities flow.

Mark is currently working on his next book, *Paradise (Re)Discovered: Authenticity in a New World*, an invitation to explore belonging, courage, and the creation of paradise even in times of uncertainty.

He warmly invites you to connect, share your story, and cross the threshold into your own becoming at https://drmarkarcuri.com.

instagram.com/drmarkarcuri

facebook.com/drmarkarcuri

linkedin.com/in/dr-mark-arcuri-alignmentcoach